WHEN GOD ASKS

You Want Me to Do WHAT?

D.J. Andrews

ISBN 13: 978-1-910205-15-0
ISBN 10: 1-910205-15-X

CONTENTS

INTRODUCTION

FAITH COULD EASILY be one of the most misunderstood topics of all time. Now more than ever, I see gifted, anointed, capable people with a call of God on their lives, sitting idle and indifferent on the sidelines. Many have lost their zeal to walk out their faith, some due to offense or wounding while for others it's weariness, apathy, or simply because they've become disillusioned or disheartened. These are the consequences of religion, *not* the result of faith. Pain, discouragement, cruelty and empty works are *not* what the Father had in mind for His people when He sent and subsequently sacrificed His Son. He provided us with this undeserved gift, that you and I might be rescued from all that is evil, so that we might have life, and have it more abundantly.

Imagine what this world would look like if every Christ-follower was fully committed to a life of passionate faith – willing to surrender all, casting their cares on Him, knowing and trusting that their Heavenly Father would lovingly guide and direct their every step. Picture a life in which we would be liberated from sickness, pain, rejection, bitterness, negativity and mediocrity. Consider a life of freedom, a life in which the enemy's chains that seek to bind us would be forever broken, enabling us to fulfil our destinies with passion and conviction. In this world we would be empowered and released to live a life of significance, a life that matters, a life with purpose and power – Holy Spirit power! Supernatural power!

You know what? We can do it. This life is available and accessible to each one of us right now! We just need to step into it. Dreams such as these may seem lofty or elusive, but my story will prove to you that with faith, all things are possible!

After all, I am an ordinary person,
who has been blessed with an out-of-the-ordinary life,
because I have faith in an extraordinary God.

While there are those who do not understand my life and this walk, there are others who are fascinated and view it as an adventure. And really, that's what it is – an adventure in faith. Living this way is never boring. The "highs" are unlike anything you could ever imagine; they are exhilarating, inspiring and rewarding. The "lows" are painful and difficult but *all* the time there is joy because when in this place, I am living for and in complete surrender to Christ.

I've heard it said that this "ride" resembles that of a roller coaster. Although many prefer the merry-go-round, I have somehow chosen the roller coaster. While the carousel is a charming, gentle and predictable ride, I wouldn't want to stay on it for long, fearful that I'd be lulled into a state of complacency that could, potentially, thwart my eagerness and readiness to serve when and where I am called. Despite the sudden and unforeseen bumps and heart-stopping jolts associated with this ride, I've found the thrilling ones, those that take my breath away and bring life, easily overshadow the challenging twists and turns that come my way!

When asked how I ever mustered up the courage to choose this path, I have to respond by saying it's been a fairly gradual process. I didn't jump into the deep end of the pool my first time out but started at the shallow end building skill, knowledge and muscle so that over time, my faith had increased. As time has passed I've grown stronger and closer to the Lord, making it easier for me to say "yes" to God, before anything is even asked of me! It hasn't always been this way, though.

There are still occasions when I've been known to respond to requests from the Almighty with a somewhat incredulous, "You want me to do WHAT?"

But after I've had a moment to collect myself, I'm usually able to get back on track with an enthusiastic, "Yes, thanks for using me!" I can only do this because I completely and utterly trust my Lord. I want nothing more than to serve Him, love Him, and worship Him. Although there's been some rough terrain to negotiate along the way, there has also been a distinct sense of peace and freedom on this path that's challenged me to question why I wrestled so long with the decision to live this way.

Saying "yes" before knowing the assignment may sound impulsive and unwise, but it's precisely what Isaiah did when he heard the voice of the Lord saying, "Whom shall I send, and who will go ..." He replied, "Here am I! Send me" (Isaiah 6:8). By responding in this fashion, he was fully submitted to the will of God, regardless of what was required of him. My desire is to do the same.

It's about choosing to be a willing and obedient participant in the life God has ordained for me. Nothing less will do.

Although my calling and journey will look different from yours, I'm convinced that as we share what we've learned with one another, iron sharpening iron, we will grow deeper in our relationships with Christ, more rapidly. Every walk of faith, every person and every calling is unique. So while there may be differences, the same Kingdom of God is being built through our lives, which are intricately woven together according to His master plan.

It needs to be said, though, that this decision to walk by faith requires both an unwavering commitment to Him *and* a compliant and flexible approach to life. It means operating outside of our comfort zones and it expects a wilful "death" to self. Once we have postured ourselves in this completely deliberate position of humility, we need to accept the fact that we will experience discomfort. This is a "given" when choosing to live in a manner that is completely contrary to the way of the world.

Despite the many trials and obstacles that have attempted to distract me, as long as I hold tightly to God's promises while maintaining a sense of humour, I am usually able to triumph over the adversities that come my way. I'm so very thankful to know the joy of the Lord. His joy manifests itself by giving me the ability to see that which is terrifically funny in what might appear to others as being catastrophic. It's when these precious moments present themselves that I am reminded of what a blessing it is to be on this journey.

So many times when I should have been crying I have instead, found myself laughing. I have to remind myself that just as God didn't bring the Israelites through the desert for death to overtake them, neither did He direct us in the paths He has, without a purpose and a plan. Once we are able to grasp the fact that God never changes, the more easily we are able to work through the challenges that threaten to destroy us.

God remains the same,
regardless of what is going on in our lives or in our world.

It's easy to lose sight of the big picture and allow our circumstances to dictate our beliefs. We need to acknowledge that we are living in an exceptional day and age. I believe it's a time when God wants to do a new and fresh work on the earth. He is calling His followers to a higher level of obedience, to a heightened degree of faith and He requires that we be prepared to act when called. He is asking His people to serve in unusual and what might appear to be, "outlandish" ways.

As He shakes the earth and wakes us up to a fuller knowledge of Him, His will for our lives and His plans for this world, we should make every effort to be prepared. I don't know the role that you will be asked to play, but I hope if you are called to something that's out of the ordinary, you'll be encouraged in the knowledge that you are not alone. If you know people who are called, envelop them in love and empathy. Stand with them in prayer and support them in whatever way you can as they embark on their journey of faith.

As we transition into this new era of God's dealings with mankind, an abundance of supernatural faith will be required of those who are serving outside the proverbial church or missionary "box." This is both exciting and exceedingly frightening. We will need to stand strong, united, firmly rooted in the Word of God and led by the Holy Spirit, determined to bless and encourage one another as we go, ever and always listening to the voice of our Heavenly Father as we yearn to see His will done here on earth as it is in heaven.

After all, if God really is beginning a new work and people are being called to unique, peculiar and even curious works or destinations, then wouldn't it make sense that a God who loves you like crazy would want you, and those around you, to be prepared for what's ahead? Whether you acknowledge this shift or not, there *will* be a "shaking" and we *will* need to come to terms with living in and with a new "normal." My hope is that in hearing my story, you will be strengthened and encouraged to walk out your own destiny, living life to the fullest, completely sold out to Jesus!

The cry of my heart is also to see an increase in kindness, mercy and love toward one another within the body. Our community of faith must move beyond its current doctrinal prisons and into a place of compassion, freedom and love. As I share these personal insights and experiences, I pray it will produce a deeper understanding and appreciation of what it is to embrace and live your own faith adventure! Please, won't you join me for the ride of a lifetime, living on the edge, for Him?

> "Blessed are all those who put their trust in Him."
> —Psalm 1:12b

Chapter 1

A Willing Participant

Reflections

AS I BEGIN to share my journey of faith with you, I am in the "valley." You probably know, understand and have experienced the valley. It's that place where things are *not* going as planned. Life isn't progressing the way we'd hoped, and we can see that for a time we'll be residing in that dreaded place of pain, growth and disappointment.

Typically, one wouldn't venture out and share their story *while* in this condition. It would seem ludicrous to even attempt to impart words of wisdom or encouragement amidst personal pain and turmoil. After all, how can an average person with troubles of her own have anything of significance to say? Well simply put, it's not so much about what *I* have to say but rather about what *God* wants to say to you, through me. Although I haven't realized absolute victory, apparent in having climbed the highest mountain, followed every rainbow—gotta love "The Sound of Music"—and … you get the picture, but for some reason, He has chosen to use *me,* just as I am, to encourage *you*!

> God wants me to share with you, from this place of humility and brokenness, what it is to have faith in the difficult days.

1

He wants you to hear His truths from someone who isn't currently jumping for joy in a mountaintop experience. He wants you to know that He loves you and He will never leave you or forsake you from one who must remind herself of this very same thing every day.

Sometimes it can be challenging to believe these promises are true but I've come to know that despite my circumstances, God remains the same. So it is in Him, and in His Word, that I place my trust. I cannot trust my feelings. I can only trust Him.

Sadly, I have found there are very few people who understand this journey of faith, and so it has been an excruciatingly lonely walk. As a result of each and every faith step that my husband Kevin and I have been asked to take, we have lost very dear friends. These are people who didn't understand what God was asking of us and definitely didn't want to walk the road with us. Through it all, though, I've had an undeniable sense of purpose and determination that has propelled me upward, onward and toward the goal. I've been able to run the race set before me.

Hopefully, it won't be long before I emerge from this valley but in the meantime there is apparently still a great deal that I must learn while here. So, I'll do the only thing I know how to do which is to fix my eyes and heart on the Lord, seeking His face, and remain on my knees. There have been tough days before and there will be difficult days ahead. There are numerous people with stories that are far more troublesome than ours and some that aren't nearly as bad but the bottom line is this, when you're in the valley, it's really not fun.

Pain is pain. Heartache is heartache. Loss is loss.
Trying to judge another's pain is futile at best and cruel at worst.

January 1, 2008. Typically the first day of a new year is a day of new beginnings, fresh determination and hopeful anticipation for all that the future holds but today, for me, it is a day of utter desolation. Broken and crying out to God, I feel as though my heart has been shattered into a million little pieces. Our financial resources are nil. We literally have absolutely nothing with which to live. Our teenage children also have nothing because they've contributed all their savings in order to pay our rent.

I am sickened to the core by this new "low." Without a vehicle, the five of us walk, take the bus, or accept rides from generous folks. Attending meetings or functions is challenging and grocery shopping, when we have the funds to do so, is downright painful especially when considering the arduous trek home, usually executed in a rainy climate.

Our furniture, dishes and clothing are "tired," and we're continually fighting issues of mould in our home, something that's particularly challenging, given that I suffer from an auto-immune disease and a vast number of allergies. We live in a foreign country because just over three months ago, God sent us away from our homeland, family and friends, to a nation half-way across the world, to a place we'd never been, where we didn't know even one person, and He hasn't informed us as to why – yet.

Just over four weeks ago, my very precious dad—a hero of the faith and a hero of mine—passed away after having been diagnosed with cancer only two days after we arrived in this new land. Our days and nights have been filled with mourning this loss and coping with the pain of leaving my mom. Our surroundings are unfamiliar and we frequently need to battle the depression and oppression that permeates the country to which we've been sent. We have our faith and we have one another and that's it. God has stripped us, emptied us, and removed us.

Although today is a difficult day, I am clinging to the hope of tomorrow. I know that with God leading me in His gentle and compassionate way, I will eventually find my way up the rocky terrain, joyfully breathing in that mountaintop experience – having grown and experienced a fresh wind of God in my life by way of a broken spirit and a contrite heart.

For some reason, today, God wants me to share with you in this place of brokenness, what it is to have faith in the difficult days. He wants you to know the possibilities that lay ahead of you and that although you, too, may be in the valley, it's possible to move outside the confines of your own pain and add value to the life of another. This is something that I hope to do for you through my story.

As I look back on my walk, I am able to see how and why God has led me down this path in the ways and means He has. I can see how blessed I've been to live a life of purpose and passion. Naturally, we have those moments when we observe our lives through a more "worldly" lens and from that perspective, things may appear quite grim. This is why we ought to view our lives as God does – pleased by the people we have become and filled with hope by all that we are yet to become. He sees the potential and the possibilities that lie within us, not the flaws and culpabilities.

Like the gentleman He is, He patiently waits for us to discover who we are, in Him. He stands at the gate like the father of the prodigal son, in anticipation that soon we will be home - not perfect, not rich but with a renewed understanding of His strength and how desperately we need Him in order to accomplish anything of significance.

> Right here and right now, we can do mighty exploits for Him,
> knowing that in and of ourselves, it was impossible
> but with God ALL things are possible.

Choosing a life of faith can prove challenging, especially for those who need to overcome an opposing spiritual background, upbringing, or training. It may even require a major overhaul in one's thought life in order to release incorrect teaching or legalistic beliefs from the past and open ourselves to a new way of thinking. In allowing Christ to rule and reign in our hearts, it's imperative that we also give Him access to our heads, our minds.

By nature, we humans are generally resistant to change and uncomfortable with looking at life and faith from a new perspective. Sometimes we become trapped or entrenched in teaching that binds us and makes it next to impossible for us to break free. What amazes me is that we Christians expect agnostics, scientists, Muslims, Buddhists, or even our own unsaved friends, to look beyond and outside their teaching and yet we ourselves, refuse to seek God and Jesus beyond that which we have been taught. Ouch! That one may have stung, but it needed to be said.

Rest assured, although we may not have all the answers and we may not know what tomorrow holds, we do know *who* holds tomorrow. With that in mind, I am certain God, the maker of heaven and earth, is more than able to accomplish what concerns us today.

While remaining firm in Christ and in the Word of God, we must also endeavour to remain "open" to the possibility that we may have gotten some things wrong. While one church or ministry leader could espouse a certain belief, that same "core value" might be completely dismissed by another institution. Who is right? Usually we believe the truth resides with the one we are following, which is why we are following or have "bought in" to that particular body of believers. However, this can also prove dangerous.

We should only follow Christ. We should only align ourselves with Christ. This way, even if our leaders are off-track or go astray, we are still hearing from, and in line with, our Lord. The truth as I understand it today is simply that, the truth that I know *today*. Tomorrow I may have additional revelation and understanding and so, as a result, things may look a little different.

I stand before you, not as an "expert" or one to follow, but as a regular woman with some undeniably real experiences. My understanding is based simply and solely on the Word of God, revelation as I know it today and guidance as given by the Holy Spirit, and the wise counsel of those on similar journeys.

As I said before, the ride has sometimes been rough and there have been occasions when it seems as though my Lord, my knight in shining armour, hasn't arrived on time or in the ways and means I was hoping but in actuality, He always has come through for me. Not only that, but the results are usually a whole lot better than anything I could've ever imagined.

I'm also reticent to share my age, concerned it may provide a bias.

> Because this is a story of faith and lessons in the faith,
> I hope it will resonate with many, irrespective
> of age or gender, nationality or denomination.

We recognize that much of what we've been asked to do is prophetic. We are pioneers. Our story is simply a foreshadowing of what is to come – a way to provide insight and encouragement to those who will follow. We actually identify more closely with a group considerably younger than ourselves. My hope is that our story will give this group a road map of sorts and provide their circumspect parents with knowledge and understanding.

Although we appreciate and acknowledge the reason for this "call," it doesn't change the fact that I am nearly 50, my husband is nearly 60 and we are in the position of "starting over." Our peer group seems to be continually shaking their heads and rolling their eyes whenever our names are mentioned. The emotional roller coaster associated with this life of faith and my personal battles with illness have also taken their toll. While things from a worldly perspective look a little ominous, surprisingly we have remained optimistic. We still possess a youthful drive, determination, willingness, passion, and hope for all the future holds.

Once again, though, the key to having achieved this attitude has been in continually reminding ourselves to *not* look at our situation with human eyes. While this can be extraordinarily difficult to accomplish, I am determined to measure my life based on how my Heavenly Father views me, rather than through the eyes of those who judge me. It's when I see things with fleshly eyes, as the world would view me, that my life appears bleak at best. This is the key, though! I need to remain focused on "things above." I need to maintain a spiritual perspective.

It requires a lot of work and discipline to see things from God's perspective, especially when the earthly vantage point is continually before me.

It should have been a relatively simple task and yet, as a result of the heavy grocery bags lining my hands and arms, welts and a distasteful array of rashes had begun to emerge on my skin. I was trying to keep my mind off the obvious discomfort when my thoughts inadvertently meandered back to a simpler time.

These memories did not serve to placate me but merely reminded me of the insanity of my current situation. It was strange to me that I was finding solace in recalling films I'd seen of African women carrying buckets of food and water on their heads for miles and miles in the hot sun. I reprimanded myself for thinking such thoughts and wondered why it is that we must focus on someone worse off than ourselves in order to be consoled? Ah, the human condition in all its complexities.

I was shaken back into reality as one of my plastic bags broke and a package of strawberries tumbled across the sidewalk. I put everything down, scrambling to pick up as many of the berries as possible, all the while re-organizing the shopping so that it would fit into one less bag. I pushed aside thoughts of how I must appear to passers-by. No matter how you sliced it, this was highly unusual – a skilled, career-oriented, mature North American woman carrying food for a family of five, all alone, via bus and then up a steep and seemingly never-ending hill in the pouring rain to home, with so little money that not one bit of food could be lost! I couldn't recall signing up for this. Still, the physical part of the escapade had been the easy part.

The trying times had been the countless hours and days previous to this, spent in desperate and anguished prayer, waiting and believing for our empty cupboards to be filled. My heart hurt and the tears flowed freely.

So, how did I get to this place? Well, let's start at the very beginning, a very good place to start – "The Sound of Music" again?

My story is unique, just as your story is unique. That, in and of itself, is incredible to me; our stories can be so different and yet, as long as the destination is Christ, we all end up at the same place, living for Him, seeking after Him and His righteousness, and enjoying His blessings! Growing up in a Christian home, I learned early on I was loved and special and protected. I learned to pray, to read the Bible and to obey the commandments. As I grew, I discovered many others did not share the same kind of life I did. They didn't have a supportive, encouraging mother and a gentle, prayer-filled father. Their lives were, in some cases, tragic. This pained me, and out of compassion I was able to "share" my parents with others who needed at least a taste of what my brother and I had in abundance. Although we weren't financially wealthy, we also never seemed to be in need.

Days before turning age twelve, I made the decision to follow Christ, with a resolve to serve Him for the rest of my life. Of course this would not always be the case as I, like so many, would find myself at various stages in my walk, stagnant, floundering, or simply off-track. Meeting my husband Kevin is what really started to bring me back to God. The more I shared the goodness of God with him, all that I had learned while growing up and what I knew to be true, the more this faith inside of me was renewed and began to bubble up again. I realized how much I missed this relationship with my Saviour and began to thank Him for never giving up on me.

After marrying, Kevin and I began to faithfully attend church, raised a family, worked, lived and generally felt called to be salt and light, which I believe we were. Over time though, I began an even deeper journey of faith and what I encountered and learned along the way is what I would like to share with you here.

This walk has taken some staggering twists and turns
beginning with seven significant words
that forever changed my life.

With those words, God plucked me out of a stable job with the culture department in government and into an amazing adventure with Him. Since that time I have been passionately committed to, and captivated by, the power of worship evangelism – be it organizing, managing, singing, producing or directing large outreach concerts, events and festivals. I've been blessed with opportunities to do prison ministry, street ministry and uniquely mission-minded endeavours. It's been a phenomenal ride that's taken me to new depths and dimensions of this wondrous thing we call "faith."

What is Faith?

So, what exactly *is* faith? How is living *by* faith unlike living *with* faith? What is the difference between faith and religion? Why live a life of faith in a world that expresses such contempt towards those with a resolve to follow Christ? These are just a few of the many questions that could cause a person to shrink back in fear from choosing such a life. From my perspective, I can tell you, with all assurance, that faith in Christ is life-changing, world-changing and a decision that I would highly recommend.

A person of faith is one who is grounded in something much bigger, deeper, and more profound than self. The very word "faith" propels my thoughts to a place of peace, strength, power and conviction. It motivates me to look beyond myself, my environment and my circumstances.

When I speak of my faith to non-believers, they'll often revert to an assumption that I am "religious." But I am not "religious." I am filled with faith. This, to me, is considerably different. My faith isn't about law, system, structure or traditions but rather, it's about relationship. My relationship with God, with Jesus, with the Holy Spirit is as real as any other relationship I have. My confidence, my trust, is in my Lord. Yet while this faith is about relationship, its very foundational principles are based on the Word of God, the Holy Bible. So what does the Bible say about faith? The most common definition is found in Hebrews 11:1 which says, "Now faith is the substance of things hoped for, the evidence of things not seen."

This is a concept that can be difficult for us to get our minds around, but essentially it's saying that faith is about hope and beliefs and not about anything concrete or of this world. It's not something we can see or touch in the natural. It's spiritual. This is reiterated in 2 Corinthians 5:7 with Paul's simple explanation that,

"We walk by faith, not by sight."

Although seemingly straightforward, it's a concept that is lost on many. If I were listening to a comedian speaking on this subject, I would picture him wryly but comically cajoling into his microphone, "What part of *not by sight*, do you not get?" And when you think about it, he would be absolutely correct. Somehow, some way, a large percentage of the Christian community in particular has missed out on understanding what faith is all about. I think we've somehow come to believe that when we live by faith, it simply means we have a nice relationship with God, our family and our church family, yet pretty much live the same way that everyone else in the world lives. Of course we may attend church, do our best not to sin and we try to do nice things for others. But on a day-to-day basis, we don't look too much different from the world, and what's worse, people who do are considered to be strange and might even be subject to ridicule.

If faith is belief in and for something we cannot see and that is clearly scriptural, then why is it we have such difficulty understanding our brothers and sisters who are called to do something out of the ordinary – something that may not be clearly defined or may not seem "realistic" as we understand reality to be?

We've confused *having* faith with living *by* faith.

When folks witness a true walk of faith, it doesn't necessarily "fit" with their understanding, ultimately making them feel very uncomfortable. This would explain why those who criticize feel that not only should God's request make complete sense to them, but that a comprehensive plan should be attached to that request. This, to me, sounds more like a business transaction than a call to action by the Almighty! But, this is the way many have been taught to envisage faith. Because of this lack of understanding, not only are people often repelled by the very thought of what a person of faith is doing, but in some cases, they are even repelled by the actual person. I believe that what makes people so uncomfortable is the "unknown."

It's the "not being able to see" part of
the equation that bothers folks.
But faith actually means not seeing.

10

As soon as we can see, it's really not faith any more, is it? Let me repeat that ... once we can see, we're no longer operating in faith because it's not only evident to us, but to everyone around us. When that happens, it's about seeing in the natural and there's nothing supernatural or faith-like about that! This doesn't mean, however, that when that which we've "believed for" becomes visible to us, we no longer *have* faith. Hopefully that kind of faith is with us continually, as we navigate our way through life.

What's interesting, though, is that when God asks us to do something in faith that others find strange and difficult to comprehend, there is almost always an undeniable certainty and a conviction that comes within our spirit. There is a "knowing" that accompanies the request.

Now in saying this, it doesn't require the "calling" be something huge and earth-shattering. It could be anything. It could be a nudging of the Holy Spirit to take some time to pray awhile or help someone in need. It could be that you are prompted to initiate spending time with a young person who is going through a difficult time or to help an elderly or disabled friend. Maybe God is asking you to do something even more radical, like volunteer at the prison or go speak with someone who needs your forgiveness or your apology. Any of these things could strike fear into the hearts of those whom God has called out of their comfort zone. The issue is this – if you know God has asked you to do or say something and you don't know why, you have a choice. You can:

1. Listen to what He's asking of you and then do it.
2. Seek further confirmation and once received, do it.
3. Hear Him and ignore Him *or* run from Him (didn't work for Jonah, so it likely won't work for you).
4. Put yourself in a position that makes it difficult for God to speak to you. This can be accomplished by separating yourself from Him either through unbelief, sin, disobedience, lack of knowledge, understanding, faith or any number of other ways, ultimately, ignoring Him and His request or even potential requests, of you.

If you really know in your spirit that there has been a request made of you, are you going to refuse to be obedient because the reasons are not fully laid out for you? Are you concerned that you don't yet have a full understanding of the plan or, are you just going to do as you are asked? If you are a parent, then you will understand that there are many occasions when what you require of your children is simple obedience.

Sometimes there may not be time to fully explain yourself, or perhaps they don't yet have the maturity to comprehend the reasons for your requests. Bottom line, you expect that they will obey you. You need them to trust that you're not going to ask them to do something that will cause them irreparable damage. You need them to have faith that you would never, purposefully, hurt them. If they are hungry and you ask them to wait fifteen minutes until dinner is ready, you are aware that it will cause them a degree of discomfort, but that waiting won't mar them for life.

It's the same with God, who quite simply wants us to trust Him and do what is asked of us, whether or not we fully understand. It needs to be said though, that instructions from God carry with them more complicated ramifications in relation to our knowing or not knowing the whole picture. If we knew the entirety of His plans and could see what we were getting ourselves into, there's a strong likelihood that we would say "no." On the off-chance that we agreed, it's probable that we'd have the humanly arrogant tendency to attempt to "refine" the plan to suit us and our purposes.

Jesus was remarkable in so many ways but what truly blows me away is the fact that, although He was the Son of God, He was also the Son of man, having the same emotions and temptations as the rest of us.

> He not only *knew* but had to *live* with the fact,
> that His entire sinless life and existence would end in a
> horrible, painful, unjust death by crucifixion.
> He had to live with the knowledge that He would visit Hell!

I can't even comprehend what it would be like to live with this sort of knowledge and still go on with life. Although we may find it frustrating, the times when we are *not* able to see, it's likely what God knows is best. After all, if it was good enough for those great men and women of faith who have gone before us, then it should be good enough for us.

Would Moses have embarked on his forty-year journey had he known all that he would endure? I somehow doubt that many of us would have jumped to the front of the queue, hoping for this assignment. And yet, although the trials he faced were agonizing, he also witnessed miracle after miracle first-hand. He spoke with God and God spoke with Him, unlike any other. He was on the roller coaster before any such invention had been manufactured! The highs were high and the lows were low.

I've also learned that what may appear to us as our having been obedient and sacrificial is ultimately still about God providing us with a gift. When doing "our part" and things get difficult, it's tempting to pout and remind God of all that we've done for Him. Yet in the end, it's about God choosing to bless us.

> When opportunities arise to "give until it hurts,"
> we are provided with the chance to prove our faith.

This not only pleases Him but in the end, blesses us! We still win!! Others have been used mightily by God and we can be, too. It's got nothing to do with what we've done for Him and has everything to do with what He's done for us, knowing that in the end, without faith it is *impossible* to please Him.

If you find this thinking to be confusing or foreign to you, then I implore you to sit down and have a conversation with God. Ask Him to open your eyes, ears and heart to His perspective. Ask Him to reveal Himself and His ways to you, in a manner in which you will know without a shadow of a doubt that you have heard and understood.

For those who are deeper in this walk and are still grappling with "faith," then you'll likely need to re-examine your beliefs. Lay aside worldly or religious views and immerse yourself in God's. Perhaps somewhere along the way you received incorrect teaching or simply misunderstood a lesson. Ask God to help you to learn and receive His truths. It's important that you know you're not alone. It's because there are so many who don't understand faith that I was motivated to share my story.

> When Jesus said to His disciples "follow me,"
> they didn't know where they were go-
> ing or what they would be doing.
> They simply went!

When Moses wandered through the desert, he was unaware of the challenges he'd face, let alone the destination or how long it would take to get there. By faith, Abraham laid his beloved son Isaac on the altar when asked. By faith, the walls of Jericho fell down and because of faith, kingdoms were subdued and folks were raised from the dead. Now, that's pretty incredible stuff! I definitely want to be a part of these kinds of adventures. To do so, however, means refusing to allow misunderstandings or fear to stand in the way. We must be continually available, seeking after Him with a willingness to "act" when called.

I could feel the presence of the Lord in a way unlike any other. It was as though I had been transported to another place and time. My heart was bursting as I worshiped with complete abandon, captivated by His love, declaring His truths with a confidence and boldness like never before.

I wasn't in a church but in a prison. We were leading a number of incarcerated youth in a time of passionate, vulnerable, honest, transparent worship. It was one of the first times I could ever recall being completely unencumbered by formality and religious expectations. I was anointed with a freedom to sing and speak of God's goodness in a way unlike any other. Surely, this was heaven and not prison!

I was jolted back to reality as I recalled an earlier comment from one of the younger band members who jokingly inferred that these teens would not be able to relate to someone my age. Insecurity bubbled to the surface and I began to believe the 'lie." Not many minutes later, though, a number of these same teens rose to their feet, making commitments to follow Christ. I was overwhelmed and unable to conceal my joy. I erupted with, 'I'm so proud of you!' It was out of my mouth before I could stop it. I realized what a "mom" thing it had been to say.

As I internally reprimanded myself, the Lord whispered into my ear, "That's the first time many of these boys have heard that." I was greatly comforted and could see He was using me, uniquely, and that each of us has a role to play. My focus needed to remain on Him and His plans, not the thoughtless words of others.

Fear, Faith, and Love

Fear can greatly hinder us in our walk with God. What many do not realize is that faith requires courage, and courage is not the absence of fear just the ability to control it. Think of it this way:

> The definition of faith is essentially the
> same as the definition of fear.

When we live in fear, we believe that something we can't see (but fear) is going to happen. When we live by faith, we believe something we can't see (but hope for) is going to happen. Fear and faith have the same definition but they come from very different sources. They also both find a way of being fulfilled. Wherever our focus lies, and on whatever our eyes are fixed, usually dictates what comes out of our mouths and eventually what becomes of our lives. It's far better to hope and have faith for that which is good, than to live in fear over that which is evil. We need to keep our focus on Jesus.

It can get complicated though, because we are also instructed to fear the Lord. This, however, is a healthy fear. "Fear of the Lord is the beginning of wisdom" (Psalm 111:10, Proverbs 9:10).The Fear of the Lord brings: knowledge (Proverbs 1:7), confidence, safety and protection (Proverbs 14: 26, 27), riches, honour and life (Proverbs 22:4), longer life (Proverbs 10:27), and those who fear Him are watched over by Him. (Psalm 33:18). In fearing the Lord we realize that our very salvation is wrapped up in His judgment of us, of how He sees us. If we don't fear Him, then there is a chance we may not know Him as the Sovereign I AM. There is a chance we are living according to our ways and not His.

If we don't fear the Lord,
we might be relying on our own strength and that is pride.

It's startling to note that pride (excessive self-esteem; conceit) is a dangerous sin because when in this mindset, we don't see ourselves as needing the God of the universe. We don't realize that within the blink of an eye our lives could be over, because in actual fact, everything is *not* within our control. "Pride goes before destruction and a haughty spirit before a fall" (Proverbs 16:18). Pride sets us apart from God by lodging a nasty wedge between us and Him. God desires that nothing would separate us from His love.

Even so, He has provided us with free will. He wants us to know Him because we *want* to know and serve Him. When swaddled in a blanket of pride, we have made it very difficult for Him to pierce the thick covering we have wrapped around ourselves. This is not a good place to be because when in this position, we don't have a teachable spirit. We think we either know it all or have it all. Of course, one earthquake, a massive heart attack or an economic crisis, and that theory is quickly obliterated.

So rather than waiting for a tragedy, the solution is quite simple. We just need to open our hearts to the One who created us and allow His Son, our Saviour, into those parts of us that are resistant to Him so that He can love us, teach us and heal us. We need to seek His face, knowing and trusting that bit by bit, day by day, our hearts will be softened and our faith will grow.

I've noticed that some denominations focus on revering God and His sovereignty, while others emphasize Jesus as friend. Both are correct, but on one hand there's a chance that in being overly familiar and casual, we could potentially diminish His magnificence, while the other perspective could cause us to view Him as distant and out of reach. While it's true that our Lord is loving and forgiving, He is also a just and righteous judge, and as the Great I Am, deserves our love, respect, admiration, reverence and obedience.

How can we both love and fear the Lord?

Allow me to share some compelling revelation. If we fear the Lord, then we care about what He thinks and what He says. We love Him and we love His ways. We are focused on Him and on listening to Him and on pleasing Him. If we fear people and care more about what they think than what God is saying, then we have chosen to love people above loving our Lord. We have chosen their way and not His. Even if we fear something evil or demonic, we have inadvertently given it power over us. We need to give all the love and power and focus to our Lord and Saviour. We need to concentrate on God. If we take our eyes off God and instead, place them on a person or an organization whose input has taken a priority, we are expressing adoration towards them. In essence, we are saying that the person or organization is correct and God is wrong. Whoa, that's a heavy but it is truth.

On one hand, conquering this may sound quite easy but in reality, it can actually be a difficult process, especially for those who are given to "people-pleasing." I know a little about this because, although not an extreme victim of this group, I did need to triumph over this issue and still struggle with it from time to time. I started the healing process by way of a *lot* of pain and rejection. I needed to overcome caring about the way I was perceived or judged while still caring for the people who were rejecting me. This is an entirely different subject, so I won't digress. Suffice it to say, though, getting past this whole area of pleasing, fearing or loving man brought freedom but it also required discipline. We need to have God's heart and be wholly surrendered to His ways.

In scripture, when fear is mentioned in association with
the Lord, it is coupled with love and reverence.
Fear outside of the Lord is connected to and with anguish.

John 4:18, 19 says "There is no fear in love; but perfect love casts out fear, because fear involves torment ..."

Before we leave this subject, I just need to say that in discussions of this sort on faith, there are some who might feel this is simply too much to attain and they will never "get there." Others might feel a little boastful, especially those who have heard, listened and acted on promptings from the Holy Spirit. So, to clarify, let me just say right here and now that even our faith is not about us! Although people who live by faith might be admired, they must not be elevated to a place of awe. Yes, work and discipline are required but even our faith comes from above.

Jesus is the author and finisher of our faith and so He receives all the honour and all the glory. I am well aware of how imperfect I am, of all the renovations that took place (and those that still must occur) in my life to bring me to a place of faith that is pleasing to the King. I'd be in great error and sin to take any credit for what I have learned or experienced. It is God! He is the one who transforms lives. All glory belongs to Him.

Chapter 2

DISCOVERING FAITH

The Call

LIVING AN ADVENTURE in faith became my reality when, sometime around May of 1997, I heard a sermon urging us to submit ourselves and our wills completely to God and to all that He would have us be and do. Now this may not sound very significant, especially considering that I had given my life to Christ at age twelve and by the time I'd reached twenty-eight I had a pretty decent grasp of Lordship Salvation. So to finally get the idea of *complete* submission in my late 30s seemed a little late but also a little over the edge! I had always seen myself as a light in the world, living as Christ would have me live every day in my everyday world. I had never really considered giving up *complete* control. After all, God was in authority over my life but wasn't it up to me to run it? Of course it was!

Wrong! That day when I decided to give over complete control was the beginning of the ride of a lifetime, up and down and all around - like that roller coaster and yet, from here on out, always in the grip of the Father's gentle, loving, protecting and let's not forget, refining hands, always moulding, always shaping. Within days of making this commitment, I heard the voice of God. I really heard Him and *knew* He was speaking to me. This was powerful because I had experienced more than one miracle in my lifetime but this was different. He said seven simple words that changed my life.

"I want *my* music in the world."

There was no more and no less. I shared it with my husband, Kevin, but otherwise kept it to myself, mulling it over and over in my head until finally one day I got up the courage to share it with a believer from work. After getting up the nerve to tell my co-worker what I thought I'd heard and expecting, maybe even hoping, that she'd tell me I had lost my mind, instead what I got was an emphatic *"yes, this is right!"*

Four years earlier she had attended a session given by a man of God who had received three consecutive dreams from the Lord. The dreams were about how God was going to use His music to reach hearts and souls for Jesus. She promised to bring the details of the prophetic word the following day. As I listened to her speak and as she shared the power of this word from God, I knew without a shadow of a doubt I was called to this. (See Appendix 2) God was fully in control now and He had a job for little ol' me! It astounded me that the one person with whom I'd shared these words, would turn out to be the unlikely vessel He'd use to confirm the call.

I sat out on my deck, basking in the warmth of this beautiful sunny day, listening intently to the recordings given me by my co-worker. James Ryle related his three dreams known as the "Sons of Thunder" prophecy. The crackling and poor quality of the tape faded into the background of a message and a word that resonated with every fabric of my being. I was riveted by his message, as previously unarticulated words from my own heart had been given a voice. His words evoked a passion and conviction within me that I'd never previously experienced.

He described how godly producers, musicians and singers, previously "hidden" were soon going to be used for the Lord's purposes to touch the hearts and minds of those who didn't know Him. He spoke of the power of God in music, the treasured inheritances being wrongfully spent on ourselves rather than shared with the world and how evangelistic musicians would travel (with freedom and easily mobile like motorcyclists) to places and by means that others wouldn't and couldn't. He spoke of God releasing anointed worshiping warriors into the streets.

Yes! I was one of these. I knew it and was struck by the overwhelming realization that this was my purpose, my destiny and my call. My heart was racing. My soul had been dramatically awakened and I knew that my life would never again be the same.

I got into the Word and sought God in prayer. This was real! I didn't know why He had called me, only that He had called me. Sure, I had been involved in music throughout my entire life, but I didn't know anything about HIS music. I had a wide range of experience in the secular music industry – you know ... being a light but *how* exactly was I supposed to bring His music to the world? What exactly was HIS music? Who would perform? Where would they perform? Who would attend? Who would support such an endeavour? The only thing I knew for certain was that it had to be done with excellence and integrity.

There was much to be done and although there were more questions than answers, I forged ahead, led by God. At least my background consisted of having worked for years as a singer, actor and also as a professional marketing and promotions manager in the arts. This would be my starting point. I prayed and sought out experts, some of whom I already knew and some of whom I would need to meet for the first time. I was off and running, all the while continuing on with my full time job in communications within the government.

Finally, after considering, pursuing and eventually finding no real understanding, support or unity from within the institutionalized church, I felt the best way to move forward was to venture out and produce the concerts myself under an already established business – one I had initiated a few years prior. I was fully aware of what a massive undertaking it would be, but I had run out of partnership options and was compelled to obey the call. I was starting from scratch with everything - naming it appropriately, developing an audience, soliciting corporate sponsorship, finding volunteers and deciding what "it" would be. Finally "it" was birthed – a series of Christian concerts to take place in a number of professional venues of varying sizes throughout the city. Prior to this time Christian concerts had usually taken place in churches, and attendees generally belonged to the host church.

> I was resolute in my decision to be completely inclusive,
> ensuring that absolutely every person - churched,
> un-churched, believers, non-believers, young and old - would
> feel comfortable and welcome and not threatened in any way.

For this reason, I decided to book mainstream halls exclusively. Of course, this would significantly increase my costs but I couldn't fathom doing it any other way. Nearly everything was in place! It was exciting and frightening all at the same time.

After approximately five months of preparation, the labour had intensified and I was running on empty. I requested that my full time government position hours be cut down and, against all logic and governing rules, it was granted me! This was the favour of the Lord. Still, I knew another huge step of faith was upon us.

> We needed to sell our home before we could proceed.

Without the "stability" associated with a full time job (and with my husband being a self-employed musician), it was imperative that we be free from debt. The sale of our home didn't mean we would be particularly liquid, but at least the burden of debt would be lifted. We looked for an appropriate home to rent and God provided. As a matter of fact, He provided a home twice the size of the one released and one large enough to give the company an office. Up until this time, I had worked in the master bedroom of our tiny duplex. This was another gift from God and we were ecstatic!

Our steps of faith were clearly being blessed, giving us the courage and fortitude to move forward. I was entering unfamiliar territory not only as a producer, but also as a promoter. I was just one of two professional Gospel music promoters in all of Canada and, lonely or not, prepared or not, January 23, 1998 marked our very first performance.

There were many incredible moments to celebrate as a result of this premier event, and yet I struggled with disappointment over the size of the crowd. In faith, I had anticipated that we'd have a full house. We did have a good-sized crowd but it wasn't a full house. I hadn't counted on this. I became fixated on the potential loss in revenue. It was the beginning of a very steep and often painful learning curve for me. What did become apparent was that the show itself was just one piece of the plan.

This was never more evident than when I tried, in my own strength, to garner media attention to promote the concerts. It's important to note here that media relations had been my world for the previous decade. For this reason, I had mistakenly relied upon my own expertise! Imagine my surprise when there were *no* responses from the media to cover the concerts! Horrified and humbled, I got on my knees and *while* praying, the phone rang. It was the largest newspaper in the city calling to arrange an interview! Then ... the media floodgates opened!

The artist appearing in my first concert was an icon, a Grammy winner, a friend to Elvis Presley. While doing a taped interview at a local radio station, another host was so enthused to discover he was in the building that he "sent" for him and requested that he do a live interview as soon as he finished the first one. He agreed.

As I glanced at the clock on the wall, I realized we had been at the radio station longer than anticipated. I dashed outside to pop more money into the parking metre, hoping I would beat the attendant there and avoid getting a ticket. I made it! With a sigh of relief, I strolled back to the studio.

As I re-entered the building, I noticed something had changed. Even though it had only been a few minutes, the atmosphere was different. The receptionist at the front desk had tears in her eyes and the music that was playing wasn't the usual fare. It was a song of declaration and it was captivating the attention of all who were in the building. Then it hit me; it was my artist. He was singing an impromptu, hauntingly beautiful, a cappella version of "His Eye is on the Sparrow."

I worked my way back to the studio, compelled by the faces I saw along the way. Most had stopped working and were just standing still as though frozen, quietly listening to him sing. It was stunning. With all the planning in the world, I couldn't have orchestrated anything so wonderful. It was amazing and anointed, and it was God!

A similar moment occurred when, after being interviewed on a popular morning television show, the host was so taken by this artist that he asked him to come back the following morning to co-host the entire show! The next day was Robbie Burns day and just as they were about to dig into the haggis, the host abruptly stopped to ask our artist if he would like to say grace. Naturally, he did, and hopefully so did thousands of viewers!

> I was astonished by how God was using the mainstream media to accomplish His purposes.

His music was in the world, in a professional venue but also in print, on radio and on television. Who'd have thought? Maybe only a few hundred were at the event but thousands were being introduced to Him through the media. God was using the mainstream press more powerfully and creatively than I could have ever imagined. Thank God: He is the one in control!

Just one month after the first show, we mounted our second. This time I really went out on a limb, by producing the event in a well-known local hot spot, a night club that was known for drawing world-class musicians. This decision to bring His music to the people - all people - was in direct response to the great commission to "Go into all the world." I felt strongly that it was in keeping with how Jesus would have done things, and that was good enough for me! So despite a few raised eyebrows from the more "religious" faction about the choice of venue, which by the way turned out to be brilliant, it was an outstanding evening.

A great deal happened as a result of this concert, not the least of which was the beginning of some lifelong friendships between me and a couple of the singers. The house band, of which my husband was a member, began to grow in popularity and it was evident this gifted group was a key ingredient to the success of these shows. A strong band full of professional, Christian, anointed players, all of whom were home-grown, was a huge plus!

The employees at the bar were moved beyond belief, as were the many in attendance that didn't belong to a church family. We were gaining positive recognition from the community and the media. They loved our first two events, and trust was building. Fear was being alleviated and the world was beginning to see the sincerity of our hearts. But amidst the blessings, there was also a storm brewing. The immenseness of this responsibility, combined with ongoing negative undercurrents was daunting.

We were experiencing spiritual attack like never before.

I was being hit hard with everything – illness, conflict, oppression, relational difficulties, and jealous accusations from church leaders (the majority of whom I had never even met!) My husband and I were met with the harsh reality that we had stepped out onto a battlefield. This had somehow been lost on me prior to this time.

As the season of concerts continued, the learning continued. Working with immigration, Revenue Canada, the IRS and Nashville's talent agents and management companies was an education in itself. I found it staggering that many groups chose to sing with instrumental tracks rather than with our very professional band! I felt sure that once they heard the rave reviews from those who had worked with our musicians and knew of their outstanding capabilities, they would change their minds but, sadly, this was not realized until much later.

I was very uncomfortable with this "trend" because my goal was not to be just "as good" as the shows in the world but better, and tracks would be completely unacceptable in the world. Why was it acceptable here in the Christian world? I was baffled but needed to proceed as best as I could. What this did accomplish however was to motivate me to shift my focus onto some of the outstanding *local* talent who I knew would *love* the opportunity to work with this band. It would give them an occasion to use their gifts, garner some attention, and hopefully add momentum to their music careers.

As a result, two of the shows from that season ended up featuring local artists. Not only did this tie in with my current focus but also brought to fruition an old dream. When I originally started the company, the concept was to provide a platform for both promising and established artists. I wanted to give them an opportunity to be professionally marketed and promoted in performances designed to showcase their talent. At that time, I had no idea it would be Christian music. Now, five years later, here it was. The stage was set and I was delighted by the incredible response. The live music venue was bursting at the seams filled to more than twice its capacity! This was even better than the soft-seat theatre.

There was a group of fifty accountants who had booked their table early on. Every year, they would congregate at this club to celebrate the end of tax season. Initially, they were disgruntled when they found out the evening would feature gospel music but the nightclub staff encouraged them to stay! And stay they did - all evening - and had a tremendous time, hooting and clapping throughout the entire show. They genuinely enjoyed the music, and we enjoyed the freshness of their enthusiasm.

It's encouraging to note that throughout this inaugural season of concerts, people were making decisions to follow Christ! Believe it or not, this actually bothered many of the church leaders. Go figure. In spite of the opposition, I was beginning to get a handle on what was expected of me, but was weighed down by the associated responsibility, my incredibly busy schedule, and battling a cancer scare of my own. I just kept pushing through the difficulties.

Between the concerts, my job, my church, my health, and my family, I was juggling a lot of balls. Something had to change before I dropped one.

> It was time for another leap of faith, a decision
> to completely leave my "stable" job,
> which also meant forfeiting all remaining "security."

This was extraordinarily difficult given that, although not in debt, we didn't have anything extra with which to operate. We would be fully dependent on God and on this new venture. We were primed and ready for season two. With no regular income, this meant increased pressure and some penniless and lonely times. Pioneering was more challenging than either of us had ever foreseen.

In the World

There were just two and a half months to prepare for the next season and it was grander than the first. I produced a total of ten concerts! One of the concerts was in two cities, and four of the groups were from Nashville. In keeping with my commitment to local talent, each of the headliners had a local opening act. As expected there were plenty of ups and downs throughout the season. I was growing deeper in my faith and also battling discouragement.

One of the more significant and unique things that happened here was that, despite the trepidation of a few critics, I decided to do something quite bold and hire a scaled-down version of the local professional symphony orchestra and incorporate a two-hundred-voice choir into a very significant gala event that featured the best jazz vocal group on the planet, "Take 6."

Needless to say, this attracted a lot of attention. In fact, there was so much attention, mostly positive but some controversial, that the large concert hall was filled, almost to capacity, for two performances. Incredibly, more than half of the audience came as a result of mainstream marketing! Also significant is how God used the event to provide a witness to many of the orchestral musicians and choir members on stage, those who were actually performing in the concert! Isn't that just like our loving, tender-hearted Father, to ensure that many of those who wouldn't have attended on their own were actually paid to be there and hear the gospel?!

> We were in the world but not of it and we were starting to get the hang of what it was to take the "salt and light" concept to a new level, one that involved a bolder stance, and it was rewarding.

It was also fascinating that God was using us, a "non-church" group to bring healing to the body. As we incorporated folks from various churches and organizations into these events, "harmony" was established. It wasn't unusual for forty or fifty "churches" to be represented at any given concert and that was just on stage. God was at work and the walls of resentment, hurt and indifference were coming down.

A truly memorable moment in season two was at the final concert. In sharp contrast to the previous gala, which was big and majestic, this event was quiet, introspective and intimate in nature.

A sea of people surrounded me as I stood in the lobby of the theatre after a beautiful concert featuring Australia's Michelle Tumes. An unexpected tug at my arm drew my attention away from the merchandise table as a friend frantically summoned me into the theatre.

I attempted to glean a better understanding as to the urgency of her request but as I rushed behind her through the crowd, all I heard was, "something is happening." I had no idea as to what was going on but when I entered the theatre it was as though a glow permeated the room.

A young man was on his knees, arms raised, sobbing uncontrollably while friends stood around him, praying. As I approached, he came to his feet, staggered over to me, hugged me and said, "Thank you for doing this. Thank you for what you do." This un-churched young man had been so touched by the music and the Spirit of the living God that, at the end of the concert with no prompting by the artist and no altar call, he had asked the Lord to reveal Himself to him. He wanted to know God for himself, not simply through those who had invited him. The next thing he knew, he was on his knees and Jesus was in front of him!

I couldn't get over the fact that this brand new believer had already fully grasped our hearts. He "got it." It was just as promised in the prophetic word. God was at work in and through the anointing of the music.

Having been immersed in music for most of my life, it was an easy transition to see that the anointed arts could be a powerful evangelism tool. Music and art have the unique ability to speak as a language of the spirit unlike any other. The arts are powerful in that they are able to reach out and touch people deep in their hearts before their heads have had a chance to "catch up" and analyze all that's going on.

It's extraordinary to see what can happen to the coldest and hardest of hearts when the Holy Spirit touches them through song or dance or art. Although much discussion has ensued throughout churches world-wide over all things stylistically-related, generationally-related and doctrinally-related, I would encourage folks to focus on that which is God-related. J.S. Bach said it perfectly with this statement:

> "The aim and final reason of all music should be nothing else but the glory of God and the refreshment of the spirit."

That's it! It's not about hymns versus choruses, choirs versus drums or the youth versus the seniors. It's about the spirit behind the music. It's about the spirit that's influencing the art.

> "That which is born of the flesh is flesh,
> and that which is born of the Spirit is spirit" (John 3:6).

While these concerts were ultimately about seeing the lost led to the Lord, they were also about seeing a forgotten group that I refer to as music evangelists, used in new and innovative ways. It's such an amazing witness to a non-believing musician or musician "wannabe" to hear some of the best "players" they've ever heard in a setting or environment in which it is clearly evident that these musical geniuses are Christians. What a testimony!

I've seen first-hand how powerful it is and I've seen the lost drawn to Christ as a result. While I know we are expected to reach the poor, I'm also compelled to reach those who are poor in heart and poor in spirit. Folks don't have to be poverty-stricken to need Jesus.

> The lost aren't just the drunks and the drug addicts.
> They are also the gifted and the beautiful.

The lost are lost, regardless of income or position. People of influence also need Jesus and when they decide to serve Him, they can take their passion and drive for excellence and use it to effect positive change for the Kingdom. With Christ in them, they will live a life of even greater significance than before. People like this are integral to prompting real and lasting change in our world. These "influencers" must be reassured that when living for Christ they don't need to take steps backward, but that they should continue on in achieving superior workmanship, promoting godly change in a world that needs the hope that comes from knowing Jesus.

People in the world are watching us and so we must maintain pure and clean hearts that are right with God, consistent and in line with His Word, being distinctly set apart in all we say and do. That's a tall order but a goal worth realizing. I have been blessed with the opportunity to work with some of the finest internationally-renowned mainstream artists out there and I did it to the best of my ability. When turning my sights to His music, I never wanted to give God any less than I'd given to the rest but rather, more!! It is an honour to serve Him and to do so skilfully and whole-heartedly.

With the third season of concerts we experienced unbelievable financial hardships and were also blessed with unfathomable spiritual success. As I ruminated on where we'd been and where we were going, I was reminded of the purpose behind this effort.

We were here to bring God's Word, through
music, to the lost, to the hurting, to those who
didn't know Him. This was the goal.

I had to keep this my focus. I could see what God was doing with me spiritually. I had changed. It wasn't enough to put on a great "outreach" show. I *really* wanted to see the lost, saved. My desire to be in the will of God was overshadowing my need to balance the books.

God was asking me to bring even more to the table "'til it hurt," which it did. I needed to trust Him completely, which I was attempting but not always successful in achieving. He wanted me to see what was happening on a spiritual level. He was giving me words of knowledge and wisdom, visions and strange new gifts. I guess it's not surprising that as I grew closer to Him, the further some of my friends seemed to be from me. It was a confusing and difficult time as I waded through, and processed, all that was happening to me.

It was also time to ask myself some pointed questions. How many non-believing people were attending the concerts on their own initiative? How many could afford these events? How many were actually being invited by believers, which had been our original hope? Although we'd seen great success, I knew God wanted more. If they weren't coming to us, then we needed to go to them, to the highways and byways! After all, this entire initiative was about the lost, so we had to ensure that they were reached.

We began a phone blitz for that entire season, inviting people from the inner city, various missions, pregnancy counselling centres, women's shelters and the like, determined to give away at least ten percent of our seats, and what happened next was astounding; they arrived ... in droves! Hundreds of non-believers attended concerts in two major Canadian cities over that season. It was astonishing to see how moved they were, not just by the music, not just by the fact that we cared enough to invite them, but most significantly because of the work of the Holy Spirit.

At our first event of the third season, there was one woman, who had not shown emotion in ten years who experienced incredible breakthrough. One of the workers from a pregnancy counselling centre testified that one of their young clients had decided *not* to abort her unborn child, scheduled for the following day! One of my more dedicated volunteers was greatly moved by an elderly homeless man who had never been to an event like this before. He had done his utmost to dress up for the occasion and although his jacket was worn and wrinkled, his face shone.

> There was healing, saved souls and saved lives and
> God's will was being accomplished. What a ride!
> This was most assuredly worth all the pain.

The spiritual activity was inspiring but we were greatly disheartened by the amount of money we were losing. So often I had heard the phrase "God's will. God's bill." So why were we struggling?

I was in the midst of running errands a couple of days prior to the next concert when I had a truly astounding vision. Strangely the entire thing happened while I was driving.

In the vision, I could see myself sitting at a table with a huge pile of money in front of me. I was guarding it, protecting it, watching over it. As I sat there, I could hear the most horrendous, blood-curdling screams I had ever heard. I looked over and saw a person literally being sucked in by huge flames. It was a horrific fire and the terror that ran through my soul was almost more than I could bear. It was truly frightening!

For a very brief second in the vision, I had thought to myself, "If I leave to go help, then the money will surely be taken but if I don't leave, the people will most definitely die." I jumped up and ran over to pull them out of the fire. When I returned, the money was gone. That was the end of the vision. My heart was racing and my body was shaking as I pulled over to the side of the road.

This was clearly a word from the Lord.

I knew my financial woes were nothing, not a concern.
I needed to focus my energies on allowing God to use me so that,
regardless of the cost, people might be saved from hell.

This was the first time in my life I had a deeper understanding of how immensely horrible hell is and that it is a place I would not wish on my worst enemy. I also knew we should be sharing Jesus more, praying for the lost, believing for more miracles.

People need Jesus. Someone needed to tell them
about Jesus. Someone needed to decide that they
were more concerned with seeing souls set free, than
their own potential rejection or personal loss.

So all this having been said, when the next group to perform arrived, we discussed the whole idea of an "altar call," something I had previously veered away from. I told them how God had spoken to me and they should do whatever they felt led to do.

Well, let me just say, of the hundreds of people we gave tickets to, most stood up and gave their lives to Christ those nights! One particularly touching image that's engraved in my memory was the sight of an entire family who stood together at their seats, hand in hand, weeping, as they committed to live out their days for Christ. I was seeing something I hadn't seen before on this scale. People wanted to be saved. They wanted freedom. This was miraculous. This was significant. This was the purpose. It was all coming together and although there were hardships, God was with us.

As I prayed for direction in relation to our fourth season, He made it clear we were to stop. We were not to continue down the same path but needed to pause and await further instruction on "the plan." In retrospect, I think what happened here was not so much about refining "the plan" but rather refining me.

My walk at this point had been more of a sprint and I realize now that God wanted me to slow down. At the time it was devastating because we were on a roll and now He was asking us to stop. Rather than seeing it as a gift, I saw it as punishment. It made no sense to me until much later. Sure, I had made errors along the way and so it was easy to believe God was angry with me. Others fed into this mindset, which only added to my deep sorrow. Of course, once my thinking cleared, I knew that in Christ, there is therefore, now no condemnation. Although He may correct us, it's not because He is angry with us but because He loves us.

Along with refinement, He was seeing to it that I grew in my knowledge of the Word, that I rested and re-gained my health. I was obedient but also terribly frustrated - feeling "stuck" but hearing His voice well enough to know I was right where I was supposed to be. There was spiritual growth and continued confirmation that God would use music to reach souls, and that was encouraging. I had lived in the miraculous and I couldn't imagine going back to the way life had been before "the call." The painful lesson learned here, was

> I was here for God and His purposes
> and not the other way around.

If I needed to rest for a season, then so be it. If it was time to pause and reflect, then it was time to pause and reflect regardless of my thoughts and feelings on the subject. God is so patient. Even though we can revert to behaving like self-absorbed, impatient two-year-olds wanting what we want, the way we want it, when we want it, how we want it, He remains loving and long-suffering toward us!

In the end, although stubborn as a mule, I did release the ministry, knowing all too well that it was His ministry and not mine, His will and not mine.

HIS Will

So, what is God's will? I've heard it said that the only way to make certain we are in the centre of God's perfect will for our lives is to go to the centre of God's perfect Word. The verse that's right in the centre of the Bible is Psalm 118:8: "It is better to trust in the Lord than to put confidence in man."

This is also what Paul speaks of in Romans 12:2 when he says "and do not be conformed to this world, but be transformed by the renewing of your mind, that you may prove what is that good and acceptable and perfect will of God." This doesn't happen overnight, although with God all things are possible.

> This happens when we allow Him, day by day,
> to re-train our minds so that, over time, we
> think more like God than like the world.

The more input we receive from the world, the more we think like the world and the more we become like the world. However, the more we immerse ourselves in God, the more we will become like God.

When Jesus taught us to pray He used the words, "Your will be done - on earth as it is in heaven." To me, this is saying God wants us to live here on earth according to His way, the way in which we'd picture life in heaven. Having not been there myself, I would have to presume this means living a life filled with love, hope, peace, joy, esteeming others above ourselves, ever and always worshiping our King, exalting the name of Jesus with reckless abandon, fully engaged in an intimate relationship with Him.

The best way to do this is to make a concerted effort towards learning how God operates, how He thinks, His perspective. We have to grab hold of what is important to Him, which inevitably will be completely contrary to the way of the world, or the way we've likely been taught. As we do this and we grow closer to Him, the specifics of our roles will be revealed to us.

We should also become aware of the strengths, gifts, talents, and passions He has placed within us, paying particular attention to the environments and situations in which we excel. Once we've done our part by developing our skills and serving in obedience and we think we've sorted it all out, we mustn't be surprised when God stretches us into areas we hadn't originally considered. He's like that!

> He'll rarely ask us to do something we could do without Him.

So in pushing us and stretching us, He's sure to keep us close because we know full well we are unable to do what He's asked of us in our own strength. Once we realize how desperately we need Him in order to accomplish an assigned task, then we're in a good place. It's also crucial that we develop a more intimate walk with the Holy Spirit. He is the one Jesus left behind to guide and counsel us, and so His role is hugely significant to walking in power!

As we learn to hear His voice, we will grow in our understanding of the will God has for our lives. Because each person and each situation is unique it's nearly impossible to determine what will happen and in what order, so try to view it as an ongoing process.

If at first, you can't seem to "hear" His voice then spend more quiet time with Him; read the Word, pray and also say nothing at all. Invite the Holy Spirit to speak to you and to minister to you, being solely attuned to Him. Permit yourself the time to just soak Him in. You may not hear anything right away but I'm confident that over time, you will. After all, we reap that which we sow. This is a biblical principle and God keeps His word. So even if, in the beginning, it is just a faint, small, still voice or perhaps a prompting or urging that comes by way of the Holy Spirit, keep listening, believing in faith that you will perceive what the Lord is saying.

You may begin to sense that something is being said or asked of you and then mistakenly attribute it to the cheese pizza you ate the evening prior! Don't be too quick to dismiss these things. Talk to God and ask for confirmation and clarification. Over time, you will find that your "hearing" is improving and that day by day, step by step, you are moving into your purpose. Of course it needs to be said that only Moses got a burning bush. Some receive dreams, some visions, some hear audibly, while others get a powerful "sense." How and when He speaks is as unique as we are and as creative as He is.

I must go back once again to the bigger picture in association with His will because Jesus also said "this is the will of Him who sent me, that everyone who sees the Son and believes in Him may have everlasting life; and I will raise him up at the last day" (John 6:40).

In the end, in order to be in His will, we must believe.

We must have faith. It seems simple. It's an easy concept so then, once again, why has it become so difficult and complicated? I think it's because of all that we're up against. Have you ever wondered why so much effort and energy has gone into attempts to disprove and discredit Jesus? Why is it that there's very little blasphemy going on when it comes to Mohammed, Allah, Buddha or Joseph Smith?

It's because the only one that concerns the enemy is Jesus.

The devil knows Jesus is the only road to God and to eternal life with Him. Jesus is the way, the truth and the life. He is the only one who threatens the devil in his quest for souls. He is the only one that Satan must deter folks from following. Don't be deceived! Think about it. Pray about it. The will of God is that you believe in Jesus, that you have faith in Him, and this faith will save you.

> "Preach the word! Be ready in season and out of season.
> Convince, rebuke, exhort, with all longsuffering and
> teaching. For the time will come when they will not
> endure sound doctrine, but according to their own
> desires, because they have itching ears, they will heap
> up for themselves teachers; and they will turn their ears
> away from the truth, and be turned aside to fables."
> —2 Timothy 4:2-4

We see people being misled all the time. How sad when people start to trust talk show hosts, biased journalists and random bloggers above our Heavenly Father. We must be strong and of good courage. If initially the assignments God gives appear small and seemingly unimportant, they're not. If they matter to Him, they should matter to us.

Chapter 3

HOLDING ONTO FAITH

HIS Word

ONE OF THE most important things I have learned and tend to repeat is that in order to truly understand what the reality of living by faith looks like, one must get into the Word of God. There is a gap that needs to be bridged between those who are living by faith, those who have faith (but think that some of us have simply taken it too far), and those who really don't understand the faith journey at all. It is here that I am hoping to shed a little light on how to get faith.

As we dig into what the scriptures have to say, we are met with our very first significant stumbling block to moving forward. This may sound blunt but if the truth be told, I've found that many who question or criticize this walk do not actually read their Bibles and those who do, frequently do not have a revelation of the scriptures that comes by way of Holy Spirit understanding. This is where things can get messy because it has the potential to sound judgmental, which is not intended. What I am trying to say is that the basis of my faith comes from the Word of God. While many call themselves Christians, not all are personally familiar with what the Bible says. Reading the Bible brings knowledge and when the Holy Spirit gets involved, revelation increases as does understanding. "So then faith comes by hearing, and hearing by the word of God" (Romans 10:17).

> This means that the only way to get faith is to know God,
> and the primary way to know God is through
> His Word and the Holy Spirit.

Because we are also encouraged to seek godly counsel, we need to make certain that the people who are speaking into our lives are absolutely offering us godly advice or insight. We should know our advisors are in the Word and that they are hearing from God. We must make certain what they are saying to us lines up with scripture, which means, that we ourselves must know scripture. "Blessed is the man who walks not in the counsel of the ungodly, nor stands in the path of sinners, nor sits in the seat of the scornful; but his delight is in the law of the Lord, and in His law he meditates day and night" Psalm 1:1-2.

> If you don't know what the Word of God says, it will be
> exceedingly difficult for you to know if the advice you are
> receiving or the preaching you are hearing
> is from the Lord.

We need to make it our responsibility to learn His Word, His teachings, His ways, and His voice for ourselves. If our only education is by way of other people, it can prove dangerous because even preachers and teachers can be off-track. You'll never know if you're receiving false teaching if you're not familiar with the truth. It's all a process and a journey, one step at a time. Still, you need to actually take those steps. So I encourage you to get into the Word and get faith!

Now for those who have read the Bible, have you ever really stopped to think about these people of faith whose stories you have read, as real people and not as fictional characters in a fairy tale? Have you thought about how they must have felt when asked by God to do seemingly outrageous things for Him? Have you considered the uniqueness of each of their stories? In other words, not program-oriented nor constrained by tradition or culture but tailored by God to suit His plans and purposes, completely and uniquely ordained and designed by Him.

Have you read about and contemplated the faith of Daniel, Joshua, Abraham, Moses, Paul, John the Baptist and Jesus' disciples? Have you read about what was asked of them and then really, really thought about it? Have you truly reflected on what it means to be called to live by faith?

> Sometimes it's easy to imagine or believe that
> if we were the ones living in biblical times, we
> would have made the correct choices.

With that said, we have the distinct advantage of skipping on ahead to the end of each story to see how things turned out. We are able to easily identify the errors these folks made along the way because we can see the whole picture. They couldn't. Again, just like today, not everyone in biblical times was called to the same thing, but those who were called to live an extreme measure of faith had a difficult road to travel!

> Those who are called to live this sort of
> faith need support, not criticism.

What I've discovered as I read in God's Word about those who have gone before, about those whom God has called to live in ways that are completely foreign to those around them is that after all these hundreds and thousands of years, not all that much has changed! There are still people asked by God to do what looks, to the world and to the church, to be completely crazy. There are still people who obey God. There are still people who are confused by the actions of the obedient, and those who mock. Same old, same old. If you want to begin to understand what drives people of faith to do what they do, then at some point, you'll absolutely need to delve into the scriptures and try to put yourself into the shoes of the people used by God in this way in the past. Although it can be sad and even difficult to hear of the trauma, martyrdom, hardships, and pain endured, especially by those who had lived faith-filled, obedient lives, it will bring increased understanding.

Let's take, for example, Job's life. One must really wonder why God allowed Satan to torment this man who had been consistently faithful and obedient. God not only allowed this adversity, but was so confident in Job's faith that He encouraged Satan to try Job. Through it all, though, God's protection was on Job; He would not allow Satan to take his life. Job's friends all had theories about the reasons for these trials and they were *all* wrong. There is a lesson in this!

Then there was David. Why did God love David with such fervency? David was far from perfect and had, in fact, committed some fairly significant sins, yet God had tremendous love for him. I think it's because David was passionate and real in his relationship with God. David was honest, transparent, humble, and openly confessed his sins when found to be in error.

> David's heart was true. His repentance was genuine. His worship was pure.

What about Noah? Here is someone we envision to be a godly man, faithfully serving the Lord, who as a result of his faith, was chosen and set apart to do something noteworthy. Although we might be inclined to focus on the end of that story, picturing how after so much toiling and labour, he and his family were ultimately saved from a deadly flood that completely destroyed the earth, there is so much more to this tale. Can you imagine how overwhelmed Noah and his family must have felt throughout this entire ordeal? For years Noah had suffered tremendous hardships as he endeavoured to do all that had been asked of him, likely appearing to his friends and critics as though he was either eccentric, insane or both.

Think about how incredibly tortured he was, bombarded by malicious remarks from those who watched him "waste" his days, weeks, months, years. There he was, out in the public eye, open to scrutiny 24/7, building an enormous structure meant to withstand a flood, in a world that had never seen rain! I can almost hear the whispers, the mocking and the jeers that must have haunted him. Worse yet, though, would have been the horrific assault to his senses when death surrounded him from all sides, as every corner of the earth was being ravaged by a catastrophic event unlike any other.

> Although safe inside the ark, Noah mustn't have
> felt particularly victorious as his friends and
> acquaintances were tragically dying all around him.

I'm confident he was grateful God had spared his life and those of his immediate family, but wonder at the horrors and atrocious memories of that event. I am doubtful he felt triumphant amidst so much trauma, loss and chaos. We see scaled- down versions of tragedy all the time, and subsequently question how it is that we've avoided certain death while another was not so blessed. Perhaps we are the ones who have lived the tragedy and we don't feel blessed at all. Either way these are big issues and often the answers do not come in this lifetime. We need to trust that the God of the universe knows exactly what He's doing and that He loves us with an everlasting love.

It was one of only a few intimate conversations that I can ever recall having had with my aunt. She and my uncle, a pastor, had been missionaries in Venezuela for decades. Our times together were infrequent and therefore, precious.

As we sat together during one of those rare occasions, I was struck by her candour as she spoke of her grandson, who at the age of nine had passed away. He suffered a major heart attack outside his school while waiting for the bus and died right there, in front of his teachers and classmates.

My teenage head was finding it difficult to fathom that anything good could come from such a tragedy. I marvelled as she spoke of her undeniable peace and her gratitude to God for having shown mercy in taking this precious child when He had.

She was certain that He had saved her grandson from something far worse that was to transpire in the future. She was happy to know that he was safe in his Heavenly Father's arms than to, perhaps, have seen him suffer something far more dreadful, or worse yet, turn from God as an adult, causing his family to wonder if, in the end, they'd see him in glory. This way, they knew!

Now please hear me when I say absolutely every situation is different, and God is doing a different work in each of us so there is no formula or answer for why these things happen, only that they do. What I do know is that while there is much that we may not understand, we still need to come to a place of trusting that the same God who created us also loves us. There are times in this walk when we "give it our all" and yet find ourselves greatly disappointed in the outcome. Walking by faith is not easy.

Once we have come to terms with the fact that God's Word is truth and God's way is the only way, we are in a far better position to serve. When folks grumble about the associated challenges, I remind them that it's not about them.

> We have a very real responsibility to push past the obstacles,
> for the sake of those who will follow.

We have children, grandchildren, and great grandchildren who are counting on us to leave them a rich spiritual heritage. Scripture emphasizes the significant impact of our actions, both good and bad, on future generations. It also clearly speaks to the actions of those who've gone before and how their decisions can affect us. This goes all the way back to the ramifications of the sins of Adam and Eve and the obedience of Noah! There is more at stake than just us!! If you are a first generation Christian, there is likely a *lot* of spiritual cleaning that needs to be done in comparison to one who is a third or fourth generation Christian. For the latter, much good has likely preceded us and we are reaping, even if blissfully unaware, the benefits of having been born into a Christian family.

The way I see it, the more I can do to leave a blessed spiritual inheritance to those who follow, the better. Even if you don't have children, there is still a responsibility to leave this world better than it was before you showed up! Break curses, pray for the land and the lost, for orphaned children and lonely widows. See who, and what, God puts in your path and how you might make a difference to those people, communities or nations. God can and will use you!

From my own experience, I recall being asked by God to guide and mentor a young woman who was struggling with a number of issues. At the time, I was coming down off the high of having seen nearly a thousand souls saved and I was focused on doing the "big" stuff, but I agreed to this assignment. As the months and years passed, I could see growth in this young woman and it was gratifying to know that God had given me an opportunity to make a difference in her life.

> He taught me what it is to disciple,
> what it is to help a person grow from
> infancy to maturity in the faith.

Participating in the process gave me joy and satisfaction, demonstrating to me that whatever the role, it's an important role. Whether one life was changed or a few hundred souls were saved, it's about living in obedience to the King.

As I sought to do His will I longed to be used by God in any way possible. I became like a sponge, soaking and gleaning all that I could from whomever was willing to share. At first glance this might appear to be a good thing but it wasn't, primarily because of my somewhat random and indiscriminate choices in terms of those from whom I chose to receive this education. Although well-intentioned, the advice given from one often conflicted with the advice from another and in some cases the counsel given was completely contrary to scripture. I found myself in a bit of a "quandary" for want of a better word. Clarity came as I became stronger in knowledge and understanding by way of the Word.

As I became more deeply rooted in faith, I was no longer tossed to and fro by various opinions, teachings, and doctrines. It's so important to become grounded in the Word as soon as possible so that we are able to hold fast to truth. Then Scripture tells us to add to that faith virtue, knowledge, self-control, perseverance, godliness, brotherly kindness, and love. We're even promised that if we diligently abide by these guidelines, we will never stumble. That's definitely the best advice, ever! When secure in our faith, it becomes far easier to hear from and trust in God.

HIS Way

And so, having grown in faith, trusted in the Lord and acted in obedience through the releasing of the business (actually a ministry), it was an *ending* to a three-and-a-half-year run of evangelistic concerts and the beginning of something new.

I wasn't quite sure what the something new would be. However, once the decision had been made to *not* continue down the same road with the concerts, but to stop and seek God and *His* plan, came the waiting, the associated frustration and even despair. I created and founded a charitable trust through which ministry opportunities could be birthed but otherwise found this to be a very quiet season. Nine long months would pass with no real visible movement. There was spiritual growth. There was continued confirmation that God would use music to reach souls. There was opportunity for me to sing again, and this was an incredible gift considering I had been unable to sing for years due to stage anxiety issues that sharply halted my opera career in the late eighties.

Then, it happened. I received a phone call. It was one of the music directors, Tom Howard (R.I.P.) from Nashville, saying he'd like to come back to Canada to record a CD and wanted to work with our fabulous two hundred-voice choir, soloists, and house band! At long last, there was light at the end of the tunnel.

We agreed to do something mutually beneficial, although I'm fairly certain that, thanks to his gracious offer, my benefit was far greater. We were able to plan for their recording and then our concert. The latter would take the form of a worship gala, which would give us the means to present to the believing community the rationale behind what had been accomplished in the past and also the opportunity to share our dreams for the future. I not only wanted to relate the vision God had placed on my heart to the people of our city, but also bring praise and worship to the One at the centre of that vision.

In short, the whole worship gala from beginning to end was of God. Everything from the date it was held (the middle of a world games sporting event) to the location (central to the games and the city) to those involved (multiple churches represented thereby seeing unity) to absolutely everything! I had waited, not always patiently, and then God had spoken and it was all completely wonderful just as promised in Psalm 27:14: "Wait on the Lord; be of good courage, and He shall strengthen your heart; Wait, I say, on the Lord!"

> But my faith was tested by a phone call
> that brought me to my knees.

There were only a few days to go until show time. Customarily, I was known to keep a watchful eye on ticket sales but because the event had been fully sponsored and we had so many participants involved in the production, I hadn't stewed over sales as had been my usual way.

You see, participants generally aid in filling the venue by inviting their friends. The hall I'd booked for the concert was a magnificent, brand new 1600-seat, state-of-the-art, theatre that was managed by a good friend of mine. I was completely stunned when my colleague from the concert hall called to advise me that only sixty tickets had been sold and would I like to cancel the event?! I was so taken aback that I could barely speak.

I managed to eke out some sort of a response but the shock of what he'd just said, stopped me dead in my tracks. I couldn't fathom that this was happening. Disappointment ... discouragement ... and embarrassment enveloped me. My mind raced as I considered the worst case scenario. If I chose to proceed, it would mean having more than three times as many people on the stage than in the audience! I was horrified. My stomach was in my throat.

And so here I was, faced yet again with another step of faith. If this truly was of God, and only sixty people were to be there, then who was I to shut it down? I had to push pride and humiliation aside and although career suicide was staring me straight in the face, it was evident that this was not my decision to make.

Keep in mind I'd had to "believe" for miracles before (in terms of warm bodies in seats) and although other miracles had been realized, not always the ones associated with the warm bodies. So, that having been said, I was quite literally believing for the best and yet preparing for the worst, knowing that at the end of the day, it would be God's vision realized and not necessarily mine.

I was keenly aware that God resists the proud, but gives grace to the humble and I needed to humble myself. My faith needed to be in God and in His work being accomplished, and not in the number of people who may or may not show up! Although this might not sound like a very big deal, it was a challenging obstacle to overcome.

There were many colleagues from the world who were watching this with a critical eye and unfortunately, even more critics from within Christian circles, most of whom had already given up on me! Well, I have to say, not only was God's presence felt by those on stage but also by the eleven hundred plus people who attended that evening. They were lined up all around the concert hall outside the building, clamouring for tickets. As a matter of fact, we had to start the gala late in order to get everyone into the venue!

As I reflect back on it, this evening was also the beginning of His separating the wheat from the chaff; those who saw God in all of this, and those who looked upon it with worldly or fleshly eyes and could not see, as if blinded by some sort of jealousy or pride. God was clearly present and yet the nay-sayers, with cynicism and judgment in their hearts, had made up their minds about me and about this ministry. What followed was truly ugly and vicious, as gossip and rumours abounded. It was painful beyond belief and I almost didn't make it out. But, as only God can do,

He in all grace and mercy made me stronger
with even greater conviction that
although grievous at times, this walk
of faith greatly pleased Him.

Many of my friends had rejected me. My husband was working out of town. It was me, my small children and very few faithful friends. I was alone. I mourned and something inside me died. I threw myself into praying and reading the Word. I was consumed by God and His goodness and a growing, insatiable desire to go deeper. In spite of all the criticism, or perhaps as a result of it, I was emerging stronger than ever. My perseverance in the faith was being rewarded and I began to recognize that as faith grows, we might be entrusted with a vision. When this happens we'll know Him well enough to know that it's *Him* speaking.

Hearing, seeing or sensing an undeniable message is where the real fun begins! When He places these jewels into our hearts, we can rest assured that in due season, His promises will be fulfilled. Although not all the patriarchs were able to see these visions, dreams, and promises through to completion in their lifetimes, how beautiful it is when blessed by God with the opportunity to witness His vision unfold before us!

I am one of the blessed, having observed
the fulfilment of many a promise.

On this particular occasion, however, prior to that glorious time, I was required to live and move amongst those who had turned their backs on our family. This meant facing rejection over and over again, each and every week at church, without being released to move on. Throughout this time of suffering, I was given a greater understanding and appreciation of the pain Jesus endured at the betrayal of Judas, and even more so by the denial of His dear friend, Peter. It was incredibly agonizing. I drew my strength from my faith and experienced some mighty miracles.

I continued to sing and was blessed to lead a music ministry that frequently visited a maximum security prison for young offenders.

We served there for about three years, ultimately seeing quite a large number of youth come to Christ. It was freeing to be there and to minister to these kids. Strangely, there was far more love at the prison than at the church I attended.

Although I was completely aware that many of the crimes executed were cruel and heinous acts, I chose to remain focused on the broken hearts and souls before me. A large percentage of these kids had foetal alcohol syndrome (something imposed upon them in the womb by their drinking mothers) and even more of them had been sexually abused (also something inflicted upon them). Their young lives had been wracked with pain that had turned to anger, resulting in sin and eventually, severe punishment.

But here's the crazy part. Not only did most of them never get a fair shot at life but sadly, once in prison, many preferred this life, feeling safer and more protected in jail than they were at home. This broke my heart. Over the years of ministering there, I often felt that they helped me more than I helped them. They were so appreciative of what we were doing, craving the warmth and acceptance that we were able to provide, thanks to God's incredible grace and mercy operating in our own lives.

Over this same course of time, there remained a small group of us who continued to pray for opportunities to bring God's love, through music to the masses, in His time and in His way *just* as had been revealed to us at the very beginning through that prophetic word. And then it happened. We got the green light *and* we received *all* the funding necessary to produce a professional gospel music festival, free admission and all, bringing God's music right into the centre of a community, in a public park, within a stone's throw of a huge public market where people of every shape, size, colour, age, and background had the option to listen or not. We prayed for an event that would be simple in its goals and structure, yet excellent in its execution.

We wanted to share the love of Christ through the music.

With the purpose being so evangelistic and outreach oriented, it was a complete answer to prayer that this event could be produced with no charge, no hidden agenda, no angle, no pressure; hmm, kinda' like God's gift of redemption! Well, God put everything into motion, including the desire to pray for this in the first place!

As I said, there was miraculous funding and there were volunteers hand-picked by the King Himself. There were musicians and artists, all of whom were Canadian, all professional and loving the Lord, with a desire to reach the lost. God chose the location and the date. He touched hearts to give, participate and donate until every need was met. What a blessing to be chosen to serve on such a God-ordained event. There was prayer, and prayer, and then some more prayer as the big day approached.

The day before the festival, there was much to be done. A stage, with a roof and all, needed to be built from scratch. This meant hours of labour in the hot sun, and I mean hot sun! Heavy duty equipment had to be brought in, barrels of water from the city, with trucks of all sorts coming and going throughout the day, bringing portable toilets, tents, sound gear, lighting gear, catering gear, merchandise, security, and more. People were working and cleaning and, yes, even laughing for hours and hours until everything was ready to go the next morning. The team leaders and their crews were all absolutely amazing. Their exuberant attitudes were such a blessing because even when something didn't work out as smoothly as hoped, there was always a sense of determination, camaraderie and faith.

> It was a labour of love, and a dream and
> a prophesy come to fruition.
> God is so faithful.

It was a day of miracles, a day I have never forgotten. Thousands were in attendance and God blessed our socks off with loads of precious memories and countless treasured stories.

There was one woman in particular who caught a volunteer's attention as she sat weeping in the shade of the trees. She had awakened that morning, jumped into her car, and started driving, with no idea as to why she had done this, nor any clue as to her destination. Miraculously, this is where she ended up! Her child had recently passed away and as she sat there mourning this unimaginable loss, she was aware of Jesus' comforting presence.

We were also deeply moved by a sixteen-year-old who had been so badly beaten by his stepfather that He had suffered long-term effects mentally, physically, and spiritually. That day he experienced the beginnings of spiritual freedom as team members spent time talking and praying with him. It was inspiring to see his countenance change as the day progressed.

I was also touched by the story of a woman and her child who had been on a nearby bike path. She stopped to listen and found herself engaged in a conversation in which she openly confessed her involvement in a cult and how desperately she desired freedom. The long day ended with another young man asking how he could turn his life over to Christ. Thousands came and went throughout the day, and we witnessed perhaps one of the longest conga lines ever. Hundreds jumped to their feet to dance and sing and praise in a public park! Our prayer and book tent was constantly active, children were getting their faces painted, food was plentiful and laughter widespread. We were greatly encouraged by the opportunities bestowed upon us to share the love of Christ with those whom God had sent.

Praise be to God!
"He who calls you is faithful who also will do it."
—1 Thessalonians 5:24

Roller Coaster

At long last we were released to join a new church family and it was here, amongst these believers, that I would experience healing from the rejection previously suffered and also some wonderful teaching. Incredibly, during this period of time, I also ended up experiencing both extremes of that roller coaster ride. I'll begin with the "lows," the completely bizarre things that started happening to me physically. Out of the blue, I began to have some highly peculiar swelling occurrences. These "episodes," I'll call them, didn't take long in progressing so that, within a relatively short period of time, my entire face grew into a full-blown distorted mess. The swelling was usually so severe that I was virtually unrecognizable, even to friends.

One day, a complete stranger who had seen me in my parked vehicle, approached, offering to take me to the women's shelter because she thought I had been beaten! Sometimes one or both of my eyes would be fully swollen shut, my lips looked as though I'd had a very scary encounter with a collagen-filled needle in the hands of a mad doctor and my cheeks were so swollen that the blood vessels on my face had begun to break!

> I began to have just a small understanding of what it must do
> to a person's sense of self when struck
> with a disease like leprosy.

When looking like this, one becomes completely torn as to how to even attempt to live a normal existence. If I went out in public, I was devoid of any confidence and absolutely lacking in self-esteem. On the other hand, if I stayed inside, ensuring of course, that I steer clear of mirrors or reflective devices of any kind, then I risked falling into an incredible depression in my "woe is me, pity party for one" place of solitude.

The other obvious part of this scenario is that I was still a wife and a mother and I had responsibilities so, generally speaking, I tried to achieve balance. When things needed to get done outside my home, I simply donned a baseball cap and sun glasses and did the best I could to frighten the least number of people possible.

Throughout this season in time came many visits to the doctor, the hospital, the laboratory, the pharmacist, specialists, and essentially all the people who test, poke, prod, and medicate you to try to find out what's happening. The obvious conclusion that this was an allergic reaction did not appear to be the answer. I do have many allergies, but the medical professionals did not believe this was the reason for my extreme swelling. Then along came a new reality. The former external swelling, which could last for a week or more, didn't seem to be happening as frequently on my face but had now moved inwards and was attacking me internally.

> The good news was that I didn't look nearly so frightening, but the bad news was that it could now be life-threatening!

In the beginning I didn't know this critical (i.e. life-threatening) piece of information, so my first new encounter with this "development" was, if I do say so myself, quite comical and has, even long after the fact, caused me to chuckle at its remembrance.

The first time that I noticed something new and different was happening to me, was in the middle of the night. I awoke to discover that my tongue was swollen, really swollen! 'How odd,' I thought. 'How did I manage this? Had I bitten it in my sleep?'

I stumbled out of bed to get a closer look and what I saw in my bathroom mirror corroborated my assumptions that my tongue had, in fact, more than doubled in size! I decided to call a 24-hour medical hotline number to get their opinion. A nurse took my call and although my speech didn't possess its usual clarity, she really didn't seem troubled.

I was about to climb back into bed when it became painfully obvious that my tongue was continuing to swell. It was clear I needed to get to the hospital. I was frustrated by what a nuisance this had become. I'd spent quite a lot of time at this hospital and was growing weary of the whole situation. It wouldn't be long before my family awakened and I was keenly aware they would need to use the van – our one and only vehicle. It seemed that the least disruptive way to handle things would be for me to ride my daughter's bike over to the hospital which was only three to four kilometres away (about 2 – 2 ½ miles for the non-metric crowd) and then the rest of the family could carry on as usual. Easy! So, I got dressed, donned a helmet, and off I went.

While riding, I realized that I was deteriorating quite rapidly and had become increasingly unstable. Although my vitals were declining, I remained calm and made it to the hospital.

Now, to get the full effect here, you have to picture the nurse at the emergency reception desk watching someone cycle into the building, park her "wheels," calmly remove her helmet, and casually wander up to the desk. Naturally, she just carried on with what she was doing, not terribly concerned about the 'cyclist' in front of her.

With her head still down, she began to fill out a form for me, asking for my name. By this point, I was actually in very bad shape and couldn't even speak because my tongue was so swollen and my system was completely out of whack. Nonetheless, I made what I would consider to be a respectable attempt to say my name, which of course, was completely unrecognizable and sounded as though I had some kind of a major disability. Confused and likely annoyed, the nurse slowly raised her head as I was opening my mouth to point to the enormity of my tongue. Well, the rest is a bit of a blur.

I was pretty much thrown onto a stretcher and injected with more epinephrine than ever before or after, steroids and whatnot, nearly launching me through the roof! Between the medication, the heart and blood pressure monitoring, the oxygen and more, what I had thought to be a rather humorous, albeit annoying, predicament was not met with the same sense of amusement by the medical community. I was sympathetic to their perspective given that they nearly had to do a tracheotomy which would <u>not</u> have been good for a singer, but if you could have seen the look on the nurse's face when I arrived, it would have made you laugh, too!

Regardless, I was now moving into new territory and every episode was different than the previous one, making it very difficult to predict. Sometimes it was my throat, sometimes my oesophagus, and other times there would be swelling in some arbitrary location like my leg, arm or foot. As it turned out, I was diagnosed with something called Acute Idiopathic Angio-edema, basically a "random" skin/auto-immune type of disease that no one understands. I was determined to do whatever I could to get well, be healed, and move past this whole thing. However, as time went on, rather than being healed, the list of diseases with which I was diagnosed grew to a place of being utterly ridiculous!

To be honest, it literally felt like the enemy was trying to "take me out" and although I had my "down" days, I was determined to not allow him to mess with me! I felt a definite and growing kinship to Job.

> Throughout the course of my journey to physical healing,
> which was many years in the making, came spiritual healing.

I learned about the root causes of disease whilst becoming educated from my brother, also a follower of Christ, on the things I could do in the natural. He had spent years of study and practice in methods that had ultimately brought an end to his struggle with colitis. I went through freedom ministry, continued to speak out words of healing from scripture, turned to natural remedies, and did my utmost to maintain a positive attitude. I wasn't going to allow anything to stop me from serving God or from being a blessing to others whenever possible.

Eventually, I came to the conclusion that although I was not fully cured, my healing was in "process." Some healing is immediate, but as a friend used to say, more often than not, it's "pick and shovel healing." It takes time. Of course, I always believed that one day, it would "go," and I was resolute in my decision to never give up!

Okay, so now onto the "high" in my roller coaster ride. As the physical and spiritual healing was underway, God blessed me with an incredible opportunity. The communications position, that I had left years prior in order to pursue the gospel concerts, was with a museum within the provincial government. The museum contacted me because they were going to be having a very significant centennial celebration, complete with performances, displays, media attention, VIPs and the unveiling of a new name for the museum by Her Royal Majesty, Queen Elizabeth II, during her Royal Visit. Would I like to create and direct the event? Would I! This was just the boost I needed. After so much pain and discouragement, it was incredibly affirming to be entrusted with such a significant role!

> I was reminded of how much God wanted to bless me and that
> I was still a worthwhile vessel for His work
> and His will to be accomplished.

There was so much that happened as a result of this post that it's just too much to share here, but suffice it to say, it was a real highlight. I knew that God had strategically placed me in this position and I was privileged to stand before royalty. What an honour to be able to pray for political leaders, policing units, government and cultural organizations, with a real sense of authority attached to those prayers. It was also incredible to see how God allowed His music and message to be a part of this public event; it was a real blessing and demonstration of His favour!

If it's true that what goes up must come down, then even the highs in our life would be unpleasant because we'd be unceasingly aware of the fact that a "low" was on its way. What seems to occur more often than not is that we frequently experience both extremes of this crazy ride at the same time! In the midst of this majestic season of my life, working with and moving amidst dignitaries and royalty, our family had hit rock bottom, financially. All the concerts and events from the past, some of which had easily cost up to a hundred thousand dollars each, had caught up with us. Because the sponsorships and support hadn't materialized to the extent required and the ticket sales weren't as plenteous as hoped, we were left holding the bag.

> We had hit the end of the road and the outlook from
> where we stood was one of total devastation.

We stood firmly on the word of the Lord to act in obedience, vigilant and aware of the vision I'd received to focus on the souls and not the money. We'd seen miraculous results from the thousands of lives that had been touched. It seemed that we had done everything we could do and now, after eight long years of toiling and battling on the financial front, we were left with two options. One was a miracle and the other was bankruptcy. We held on tightly, praying for that miracle until we could literally hang on no longer. We wept and prayed, repented for our mistakes along the way, forgave those who had hurt us and blessed those who hadn't given or served when called and then, with deep sorrow, declared ourselves to be insolvent.

> When people don't obey the nudging of the Holy Spirit to
> get involved in something that God is
> doing, it hurts the whole body.

We couldn't do this alone and yet we were committed to not allow the disobedience of others stop us from doing our part. This was a hefty price to pay. Once all was said and done, we were able to recognize God's goodness, even in this. It was our year of Jubilee. We were being set free and so we thanked the Lord! I also received revelation after the fact, that this outcome had been prophesied through the vision I'd had six years earlier. Do you remember the vision of all the money being taken as people were being saved from the fire? It was all part of the plan. This insight brought incredible peace.

Throughout this journey, we repeatedly found ourselves to be experiencing both hardship and opportunity simultaneously. After my work for The Queen, I was hired to manage an event for our province's Lieutenant Governor (The Queen's representative), and then the opening of a multi-million dollar sports facility. During this same time-frame, our eldest daughter got married to a wonderful man, one she'd waited twenty-eight years to meet and marry.

It was the best of times. It was the worst of times. Even in the midst of all these trials, in the midst of lack, illness and discouragement, God was blessing us and using me to impact leaders, those whom He'd placed in my sphere of influence. It's incredible how God uses the unlikely things and people of this world to confound the wise.

Taking Ground

I strongly encourage you to pray for those in leadership, whether you support them or not, because our leaders need to be good leaders, regardless of which party, church or group they represent. To do their jobs well and to be effective for the Kingdom, they need to hear from God.

When we pray for political leaders, teachers, business leaders, youth leaders and leaders of every kind, we are interceding for them. We are praying that God's will be done, that they will hear His voice, and they will choose to love our Lord and the people they serve more than they do their own personal need to attain position, power and control. We need to pray that they will be supported, advised, encouraged and financed by godly people. We need to trust that God can and will use them to fulfil His purposes. By praying for them and blessing them rather than cursing them, we are making a difference! What's incredible is that we can do this right from the comfort of our own homes!

Maybe some of you are meant to be leaders yourselves or to walk alongside someone else who has been called. Don't discourage those who are willing to make a difference. Even if you don't agree with everything they stand for, be reminded that it is better to have a Christian holding a persuasive position within our world system than to not. Trust me when I say that our leaders receive more than enough input from the world. I've seen this first-hand and believe me, it's not pretty to watch as a mafia leader finances and influences a politician, who was unable to retain his position without the financial support this one was quick to offer. Aren't there any wealthy godly people who could have supported someone or have they all run away from the political arena?

Maybe you're not wealthy or political but instead, one who could ensure better programming on television or produce clean family movies. Perhaps you are one who is called to develop a cure or invent some sort of energy-saving device. It's like eating healthy; there need to be shops that provide good, wholesome food for this to become a viable alternative for folks. When this occurs, it is far more effective to move our business to the healthy food store than it is to picket or write letters complaining about the burger joint down the road. This is what I had tried to do through the music evangelism events.

> My desire was to produce high quality events, in
> a neutral and professional venue, providing an
> alternative to some less "healthy" choices.

I enjoyed spending my time doing this and believed that I was encouraging the world to view Christians as people who contributed and didn't just try to "ruin" everyone else's fun. This is much more effective than being seen as the "naysayers" or complainers. Picketing and petitions can have a positive effect, but aren't always the answer.

What I learned was that over time, as I became trusted by my worldly counterparts, I would be given more and more latitude, thereby giving me opportunity to effect positive change within these secular environments. I beseech you to not only lobby and petition but to initiate, provide or support godly alternatives.

If the appropriate action isn't obvious then get a group of intercessors together to pray for revelation about how God wants you to proceed. Maybe the issue or problem needs to be resolved differently than how you originally thought. Let God have His say in the matter. The enemy chips away at the moral fibre an inch at a time, so perhaps we just need to determine to regain this ground, an inch at a time.

Granted, this requires a lot more patience and is a great deal more effort than spending an afternoon with a sign, or an hour with pen in hand, but it might just be more effective. Pray that God will bring these leaders to a saving knowledge of Jesus Christ. You may think it looks hopeless, but remember, with God *all* things are possible!

Create positive change without being offensive!

I hate to say it, but as a result of political correctness, many have forgotten what or more accurately who they represent. I've worked in environments where absolutely everyone and everything was tolerated *except* Christianity. I have encountered an incredible lack of respect from people of other faiths who have made rude comments about my beliefs causing me to wonder not only at the inappropriateness of this behaviour, but by the fact that such conduct would never be accepted should the roles have been reversed.

There's a double standard at work, but regardless of how we are treated, we Christians are required to love. We are called to love everyone even though we may not agree. Loving, however, does not mean that we are to concede.

We are *never* to deny our faith.

As a matter of fact, if we deny Christ before man, He will deny us before our Heavenly Father. That is a stiff penalty. This is why church leaders need to exercise extreme discernment about which things to remain firm (God's ways, God's Word, Jesus' sacrifice, Holy Spirit leading) and which things, they need to be flexible (style, mandate, programmes, works, timing). Unfortunately many institutions have become too steeped in tradition or programs and not immersed enough in God. Others are "in touch" but have watered down the message in order to "reach out" thereby compromising their foundational principles.

A journalist friend of mine, who at the time was a new believer, visited what might be considered a "neutral" church. He was genuinely appalled and vowed never to return, noting that if he was seeking political correctness, he could have just as easily stayed at his office.

When people are seeking an encounter
with truth ... with the Lord ...
with the Holy Spirit, then they should be able to do so
in a church that calls itself Christian.

We need to do things God's way, serving and listening to God rather than people. This is precisely what I spoke of earlier. If church leaders are listening to people of influence and that influence is primarily due to their financial contributions or their societal position, then *everything* must be re-evaluated! If "funders" leave, is God big enough to take care of the needs of the church? Is He able to bring in new people who could bless the church? Could He be asking for new leadership? Should your church even exist as it has in the past or should it become a soup kitchen or a youth centre or a housing complex for the elderly or the disadvantaged? Maybe you should be operating a mission centre or a school?

With the new wave of social media, websites, blogs, internet and so on, the playing field has changed. Pay close attention to these trends. Yes, some may be "fads" but others are the beginning of a new way of life. If you fight against the wrong ones, you could become ineffective and out of touch.

Whatever it is that God is saying, it's far better to be obedient to Him and to His Word than it is to please people and receive His wrath. Let's be willing to stop and listen to the Lord and create something positive, good and godly. It won't be easy, but by doing so we can be more effective for His Kingdom work.

Chapter 4

GROWING IN FAITH

Standing Firm

TRUTHFULLY, THERE WILL be discomfort as we walk by faith but we need to push through and past the hardships that try to discourage us. If you have entered a season that feels like hell, whatever you do, don't wallow in misery there but keep moving. Keep pushing. Keep positive.

When you step up and into the things of God, the heat will inevitably get turned up. Don't let this surprise you. Although obstacles and temptations can get in the way, we must remain strong in the Lord, knowing that God is simply challenging us to grow. Over time, as we mature in the faith, we will be stronger in our resolve to stand for Him, ultimately bringing us to a place of deep and undeniable peace.

Although it may seem strange to think that when living for and in obedience to the Prince of Peace, we will experience peace within, but not necessarily in our environment, it's true!

Bear with me while I try to explain something fairly complex in relation to peace. When we live in obedience to Him, there will be things asked of us that others won't understand. As a result, division can occur.

Now, given that unity is a godly principle, this is a bit of a paradox. But here's how it works. When God asks us to speak for Him, stand for Him or simply choose Him and not dangle in a neutral zone, the harmonious equilibrium previously enjoyed, will be shaken. While it's exceedingly difficult to understand how, while attempting to live peaceably and in unity, we may end up separated from those who, at one time, were once close to us, this is reality. Sometimes it's only for a season, but in other cases, it can be for longer. It could be that we are called to walk different paths and so God needs to separate us, in order that we might fulfil our destinies. Sometimes, it could be that these relationships are unhealthy, and their removal is God's protection.

Take a moment to think back to when you first became a believer. In choosing to live for Christ, you likely didn't purposefully turn your back on old friends but probably found that over time only a few, if any, remained. Some people pulled away as you changed and sometimes you pulled away because the environment was poison to your soul. The same thing can result as we grow deeper in faith.

As we stand for Him, things will change. "Do not think that I came to bring peace on earth. I did not come to bring peace but a sword. For I have come to set a man against his father, a daughter against her mother, and a daughter-in-law against her mother-in-law" (Matthew 10:34, 35).

So, how it is that the "Prince of Peace"
didn't come to bring peace?

Well, He *did* come to bring peace: "Peace I leave with you, my peace I give to you; not as the world gives do I give to you. Let not your heart be troubled, neither let it be afraid" (John 14:27). However, in this context, He is speaking of a peace that is within us when we live for Him.

The peace He has left us is Holy Spirit peace.
That's different than the division or lack of peace that can
occur as we stand for Him and for what is right.

I couldn't believe what I was hearing. Surely I had misunderstood. Had my grandmother actually threatened me? Was she lying to me? Where had all this bigotry and hatred come from? Why was my alcoholic uncle (her son) still living with her – a woman in her eighties?

I was struggling to assimilate this peculiar new reality in which I had found myself. All I knew was that I needed to call my parents so that I could get clarity, the truth.

I was twenty-four-years-old and had received an invitation to audition for the opera department at the University of Toronto. I thought I'd round out my time in the east by catching up with my grandma. As I lay in bed at her apartment thinking about her outlandish words and actions, it struck me that I had never previously spent time alone with her. Clearly, there was a reason for this. What became painfully obvious was that unbeknownst to me my dad had been raised in a fairly hideous environment. I later discovered that for him to remain steadfast in the faith and also protect himself, his wife, and children, he needed to remove us from that which was unhealthy, and in fact vile.

I am grateful for what he did. Although he'd experienced some incredibly painful times as a result of these decisions, he stood for what was right and we all reaped the reward for his resolve by living a peaceful, happy life. Somehow he managed to honour his parents from a great distance, while protecting us and the welfare of our family from the ugliness that he'd endured while growing up. Because of his stand, my brother and I, our children, and our children's children have an even richer, purer, more Christ-like heritage! So while we all experienced inward peace, the outward ramifications of this stand created division and a lack of peace.

Every time I am given opportunity to take a stand for God,
it is actually a gift in disguise, because it allows me to grow
stronger in my faith.

What this means is that each subsequent time something is required of me, even if more difficult than anything I've previously done, it's not such a great leap because my faith has grown, making it well worth the struggle. In all that we do for our Saviour, ultimately we are the ones to receive the reward. It's actually a pretty good deal! Remember though, that if we choose *not* to stand for Him, we have, even if inadvertently, taken a stand against Him. Just as there are rewards in standing for Him, there are consequences if we don't. Each time we stand for what is right and what is godly there is an excellent chance that we will lose some friends and maybe even some family members. I'd like to share a poem with you, written by Mother Theresa, that's engraved on the wall of her home for children in Calcutta. I love how she offers encouragement to keep on fighting the good fight!

"People are often unreasonable, illogical and self-centred;
Forgive them anyway.

If you are kind, people may accuse you of selfish ulterior motives;
Be kind anyway.

If you are successful, you will win some false friends and some true enemies;
Succeed anyway.

If you are honest and frank, people may cheat you;
Be honest and frank anyway.

What you spend years building, someone could destroy overnight;
Build anyway.

If you find serenity and happiness, they may be jealous;
Be happy anyway.

The good you do today, people will often forget tomorrow;
Do good anyway.

Give the world the best you have, and it may never be enough;
Give the world the best you've got anyway.

You see, in the final analysis, it is between you and God;
It was never between you and them anyway."

Trust

> "Trust in the Lord with all your heart, and lean not on your
> own understanding, in all your ways acknowledge Him,
> and He shall direct your paths."
> (Proverbs 3: 5-6)

It's easy to see why folks find it difficult to trust. If we've been disappointed, rejected or deceived in the past, it can be challenging to let down our guard and trust because we view it as vulnerability. Remember, though, that these negative experiences of the past were with people, not God. Although some may believe that God wasn't there for them when they called on Him, I am here to declare to you that He *was* with you during those difficult days and He *is* with you now!

It's vitally important that we grasp how incredibly deeply He loves and cares for us. When we weep, He weeps and when we hurt, He hurts. There are alarming horrors that take place every day and frequently the blame for all of this is misplaced. We become angry with God rather than with Satan. We attribute these injustices to God when absolutely nothing could be further from His character. He has hopes for us, plans for us, wanting us to grow and to prosper in all things. Even when He allows tragedy, it has a purpose. The tragedies remind us that we need Him. He wants to ensure that none perish without hope, which is the very reason that He sent and subsequently sacrificed His only Son.

This was done so that you and I might be saved from all that is evil. While here on earth, we are unable to escape some of this evil but we can choose to put our hope and our trust in God. We can opt to follow Jesus, knowing that in doing so, our eternal destiny is sealed with Him, allowing us to be forever in His presence. How I'd relish being in a place where there is no more pain or suffering, no more tears, and no more anguish. His love for us is long-suffering and everlasting. Even though we falsely accuse Him, He remains steadfast in His love for us. We just need to say "yes" to that love. Then, as Christ takes up residence in our hearts and our faith is strengthened, we will begin to comprehend the "width and length and depth and height" of His love for us. (See Appendix 1)

It's crucial that we sow these truths deep into our hearts. In learning to trust, we mustn't be impatient, but content to move into this reality, one small step at a time. Then, as we learn about our Heavenly Father, His character and His ways, our growth will accelerate by leaps and bounds. Eventually, these truths will move from our heads to our hearts and over time, we will grow in Holy Spirit power. We cannot lean on our own understanding which is limited and fickle. Our "feelings" are unreliable.

> God remains the same, yesterday, today and forever.
> Now that's something and someone worth trusting!

Don't be hard on yourself. I've known the Lord for decades and while there are instances and circumstances through which I've had absolutely no difficulty trusting Him, there have been other areas that have completely challenged me. It took me years to release these concerns and burdens, eventually allowing Him to carry the load which freed me from all sorts of pain and anguish.

It's sad when you think about it, because at the very point and time that we receive His saving power, we also receive freedom, deliverance, and forgiveness bought and paid for as part of the deal. Somehow, I had managed to leave the "shop" without taking what had already been purchased, and that which rightfully belonged to me. From what I have seen, this is very common. We feel greedy taking all that God offers, realizing that the transaction isn't at all equal or fair. We can see that we're not worthy. But that's the point; it's not possible for us to be worthy. It's about God's love and grace and mercy and Jesus' sacrifice for us! It is done. It is finished. There's absolutely nothing we can add to make it more ours.

So, in not being able to "add," we sometimes leave part of it behind. We decide to forfeit peace by keeping our guilt or hang on to "works" just in case grace isn't enough. Maybe we choose to hold on to pain and nurse our hurts for awhile longer. We don't gratefully and gracefully receive the forgiveness, the healing and the freedom that's meant for us. Let's stop this silliness and grab hold of what we've been given. When in Christ, we are in victory! This is why I am able to put one foot in front of the other. It's because regardless of my circumstances, I know that God is with me every step of the way. I am never alone and neither are you. We are all on a journey, each travelling at our own pace, down the road to a more Christ-like existence. From this vantage point it's critical that we help and not hinder one another, edify and not tear down, give without reserve and love others as Christ has loved us, freely and selflessly with integrity and honour.

And so, having personally worked through and overcome many of the obstacles before me, I was at long last, emotionally and spiritually healed and ready to be used by God. It was clear in my mind and in my heart that He was going to move our family to a new location. I just didn't know when or where! For three years, I had been alert, watching and waiting for revelation. When it did at long last happen, it happened very quickly, moving us even deeper into this adventurous walk of faith.

I think what might be significant here is that although we knew that a move was inevitable, no other information had been revealed to us. What did occur, on a fairly consistent basis over this period of time, was something I'd liken to a rhythm. It was as though we were being propelled through this phase of the journey in a rather remarkable fashion, constantly sensing that we were being led, guided, and instructed in a new and different way. Over and over again, we received just one piece of information or directive at a time. There were no confirmations, only undeniable requests along with a clear expectation that obedience would follow.

> We needed to prove our faith through obedience before we would receive confirmation, which was usually only then, followed by more direction.

It was a wildly fascinating time that held a striking resemblance to a "suspense" novel, but this was no nail biting, edge-of-your seat book or film but rather, my life! While this season progressed quickly, the time leading up to this spine-tingling chapter in my life had been founded on years of passionate prayer. We had feverishly sought the Lord, died to self, and purposefully and decidedly sown into His Kingdom work.

The initial indication of impending change transpired when the folks with whom we had a housing agreement told us they had been instructed by God to sell our house. We were disappointed but not surprised given that we knew a move was in our future. Selling this home was, however, far more noteworthy than it may sound. It had been a dream-come-true for us, a blessing and an answer to years of prayer. It was a miracle and it seemed as though the likelihood of our owning another home was highly improbable and yet, with God, not impossible. While recognizing that this had been a generous gift and a truly remarkable blessing, it was also abundantly clear that we needed to hold this blessing with an open hand. We had freely received and now we were to freely give.

The house sold very quickly so I immediately jumped into packing. Our kids were busy with school and youth activities and my husband was playing with his jazz trio at a beautiful hotel in the Rocky Mountains a few hours away. It was my task to get things organized. Here's the catch, though! I didn't know where we were moving or what we'd be doing, making it extraordinarily challenging to know how or what to pack. We rented a mobile storage container, filling it with what we *thought* was most important first. Whatever didn't fit, we'd give away…. and that turned out to be a lot!

In the midst of all the activity,
I awakened one morning to hear the words: "Get passports!"

While this should have been my first clue that God was calling us away from Canada, I actually thought it was connected to a music tour for my husband or perhaps a family vacation.

Five packages of passport forms were laid out before me and I'd only just begun to fill them out when I realized a fee would be required. Exasperated by what appeared to be a waste of time, I looked heavenward and said, "Lord, we don't even have the money to apply for these! I'm pretty certain I heard you correctly so if you want us to do this, then I really need some money to come from a source that I'm not expecting and that hasn't already been allocated in our family budget, so that I can do this."

That was it. I put everything away and continued on with my packing. The very next morning, the ringing of my telephone rescued me from the mountain of boxes before me. It was a friend whom God had awakened in the night with clear instructions to present us with a financial gift.

My heart began to race, knowing full well that the gift was in relation to the passports. This was obviously important to God and so it needed to be important to me. I committed to complete the paperwork, not fully understanding why this needed to be done, only that I needed to trust the Lord and do my part. When I went down to the passport office to submit everything, I somehow ended up in the "express" line even though I'd clearly stated to the officials that I wasn't in a rush. Apparently God had a different plan and according to His plan, these papers needed to be expedited quickly!

Sure enough, we received our passports in record time. Again, as strange as it may sound, with all the distractions associated with the logistics of moving, we weren't too focused on the significance behind the passports. However, once we were out of our house and far removed from all the busyness, it was a different story.

At this point, we were keenly aware of the fact that we didn't have a home to which we could return. We also didn't know where to enrol the kids in school, for the fall and we just plain didn't know much of anything. We enlisted very few trusted friends to pray for us. Between personal revelation and that of our praying friends, we came to a consensus.

> This move was somehow connected to
> and with the land of our fathers,
> our forefathers, our ancestry.

We began to give serious consideration to a number of places within Canada which actually encompassed much of the country. Strangely, none of it sounded right. Nothing really struck a chord except for British Columbia, mostly because we had spoken many times about moving there. I started looking for work in all the locations that came to mind, hoping to receive insight, but nothing fell into place. As a matter of fact, one day when I went to the computer to begin my search for work, it was as though my fingers were frozen on the keys and I sensed God say, "–Stop, you're looking in the wrong place." What? How could I be looking in the wrong place when I was looking in so many places (in Canada)? So I tried again but the same thing happened; my fingers were frozen. With this, I stepped away from the computer.

Over the coming days, I was reminded of those words spoken by God to Abraham …

> "Get out of your country, from your kindred and from
> your father's house, to a land that I will show you … I will
> bless you … and you shall be a blessing. I will bless those
> who bless you, and I will curse him who curses you …"
> —Genesis 12:1-3

Understanding

One day not too long after this, I was having a conversation with one of our praying friends about how baffling this had become. I laughingly said, in a sort of off the cuff manner, "Well, if we're really talking ancestry, then the place we're talking about is Scotland!"

> Silence … and more silence.

Oddly enough, this actually made my spirit jump. As the days passed it really began to sink in, that what I originally thought was outlandish might actually be "it!" Most of our ancestors were from the United Kingdom. My husband had family from Antrum, Ireland, and somewhere in Scotland. My mom's parents were from Huntly, Scotland, while my dad's grandparents were from somewhere in Britain.

I won't detail absolutely every confirmation we received, but there were so many, it became ridiculous. I reflected on my childhood, much of it having been filled with all things Scottish, including ten years of performing, competing and teaching Highland Dancing. I'd even danced for Canada's Prime Minister! I'd played drums in the pipe band and my brother was a world-class piper. As incredible as all of this was, I needed to remain calm and rational. Our focus had to be on God and on what He was saying. Was this the reason we needed those passports? Hmmm ...

We began to look into how one could live and work in Scotland and discovered, of all things, Ancestry Visas! At this point, we decided to call my brother, who had actually been to Scotland, to see if we could gain some insight from him. I was a little apprehensive to tell him what we believed God was asking of us, not knowing how he would react to something so seemingly far-fetched. Instead, he completely took me aback by telling me that a few years earlier our mom had come across our grandmother's Scottish birth certificate. This "find" instigated a whole string of events that culminated in her having pulled together all the necessary documentation so that my brother could, if required, move to Scotland himself. All of this activity had taken an entire year to accomplish and I was privy to none of it!!!

At this point, my brother said, "I don't think it was for me. I think it was for you!" We were reeling! God had a plan for us and it had been in process for a very long time. Amazing! We called my mom and sure enough, she had everything.

> Absolutely all that we would require, in order to apply for
> Ancestry Visas was in my mom's possession.

That was confirmation enough for us. Once again, though, we were hit with another financial roadblock. We didn't have the funds to apply for the Visas so we prayed quite simply, "Lord if this is of you, we need the money."

I won't go into all the details, but by the afternoon of the following day, we had enough funds for the applications, the plane tickets, train tickets, the container shipping fee, a few months' rent and additional confirmation on top of all of this … all of which materialized in an unsolicited manner- other than through prayer! We were now completely and utterly awestruck. Could this really be happening? We pulled together all the paperwork for the visa applications, prayed, and couriered them off. Now I kid you not; four days later, we had Ancestry Visas in our hands for all five of us! Everything was moving at lightning speed. I started looking for work in Scotland and found two potential positions, one in Edinburgh and one in Inverness, so I applied for both.

It was time to talk to our kids. A lot of prayer had gone on prior to this moment. We believed God was preparing their hearts and that this move was as much about them, as about us, although ultimately knowing that it was, in fact, all about Him!

It was difficult to tell our eldest that she'd be left behind along with her husband and our newborn granddaughter but she calmly and peacefully not only received the news but confirmed the revelation! Then, with some trepidation, we sat down with our three teenagers. At this point something truly unheard of happened, something that could only be God.

Although the conversation almost (I stress the word "almost") went downhill at one point, the news was received far better than we could have ever hoped or imagined!! Given that we were removing our teens from all that they had ever known their tremendous attitudes were an answer to prayer! We told them that from here on out, we'd be "in it" together.

> We knew that God wanted our children to experience this
> journey of faith firsthand and wouldn't you know it,
> they took to it like ducks to water!

We shared the news with Kevin's family, his band-mates and somewhere in the midst of all of this, my parents decided to come and see us. Although the time with them was short, we savoured every moment but became concerned at my dad's mention of having found a lump in his arm. As my parents headed back home to get Dad a medical check-up, I received notification that the job for which I'd applied in Edinburgh had been awarded to another candidate. That was the bad news. The good news, however, was that I learned I had been short-listed for the job in Inverness and that I was to be interviewed via telephone. The interview went well, but I would be required to wait another two weeks before finding out whether or not I was successful. Time was running out. I was focused on the time element not only because Kevin's contract, which included our temporary home, would be coming to an end, but also the very real dilemma of getting our kids enrolled into a school.

Given that it was now completely obvious we were going to Scotland, we could see that it was time to take another step of faith. Although we hadn't yet received confirmation as to the precise location of our destination, nor did we have jobs or a home, we knew it was time to send our container of belongings. We made plans to go back to our hometown, prepared to itemize, list and move everything from the first storage unit to the overseas container.

> There was something strangely final associated
> with this seemingly radical act!

We were at a crossroads, needing to decide on a port, all the while not knowing if I had gotten the job from my recent interview. We prayed, sought God, conferred with the kids and came to the realization that just as had been our experience throughout this entire process, the next move was ours. So with that, we decided to carry on with plans to move to Inverness, Scotland, the gateway to the Highlands. If we were wrong, then we'd have our container trucked to the appropriate location once we arrived.

This was quite nerve-wracking because although we felt complete peace in terms of Scotland, we still didn't feel settled on which community. When speaking with the overseas shipping company, the agent seemed surprised when I said that we needed our things to go to Inverness. Apparently, Inverness wasn't one of the more popular ports, but she knew of it because her husband had just returned from working there and said "it was the most beautiful place" he'd ever been. What an endorsement!

This meant that another phase in the moving saga was upon us. This time we were emptying our temporary little home in the Rockies. Suffice it to say, there was a lot of coordination involved throughout the entire process, yet everything flowed better than I could have ever thought possible. There were moments, of course, when we felt overwhelmed by the sheer volume of activity (physical, emotional, and spiritual), but the underlying sense throughout this entire season was one of complete peace, calm, and protection. Because God mobilized everything so quickly, there was almost no one who knew what was happening, which turned out to be a blessing.

> This time we were able to be "quietly"
> obedient and live by faith
> without the agenda-ridden questions, unkind comments and
> spiritual attacks we'd previously experienced.

I sensed there was a protective bubble of some kind around us. I had never known anything quite like it before, but whatever it was, it was of God and it literally carried us hour by hour and day by day throughout this entire process. When the time came to actually do the container "transfer," it turned out that I was at a women's conference in a completely different city listening to a speaker from ... well ... Scotland. No, that was *not* planned, but yet further confirmation. This meant that it would just be Kevin and a few other guys to deal with the rather daunting task of moving and itemizing all that was in the storage unit.

What became truly significant about this day was the confirmation that came through one of our friends who had unexpectedly dropped by the storage lot to help with the move. In the midst of all the "grunt" work, our friend asked where the container was going. "Scotland" was Kevin's vague and elusive reply. Our friend asked him to be more specific, so Kevin sheepishly responded with,

"Inverness but we're still not sure." As soon as this fellow heard the location, he enthusiastically replied "Yes, it's Inverness, that's where you're going! God spoke to me and told me you'd be moving to Inverness, but I was not permitted to say it, only confirm it." That he did.

Once our family was reunited and back in our mountain retreat, the calls from the slightly expanded prayer team, began to pour in. They all had the same message; "You need to leave soon. Don't delay. Don't hesitate. It's not about the job; you just need to go!" We were sensing the exact same thing.

As a matter of fact, we were getting so convicted in our spirits that we were almost crawling out of our skins, knowing that the time had come to leave. We were well aware that news would travel fast and reactions would be vast and varied. We also knew there would be a plethora of criticism, just as in the past. Our biggest faith step to date would surely cause some dissention, but what we came to terms with early on was that it really didn't matter. I pictured the day when I would stand before my Father in heaven, giving my account. I imagined Him asking me, "Why didn't you obey me?" followed by my miserable reply of, "Well ... I thought everyone would think I was crazy!" I realized how pathetic this sounded and so resolved, once again, to not concern myself with the reactions of others.

I re-learned the lesson that fear of man
wasn't going to get me anywhere good or godly.

We paused for a moment to take in the beauty of the brilliant sun shimmering off the gorgeous aqua blue lake before us. It really was a stunning sight to behold. We chuckled over comments made by one of the musicians in Kevin's trio who would walk outside, stretch, look out at the gorgeous view and then, with his completely unique, dry quick-witted sense of humour, exclaim, "Wow, what a dump!" We laughed. The crystal clear lake, perfectly nestled into the comforting embrace of the Canadian Rockies, although familiar to us, was still breathtaking. I had walked this path nearly every day for eight gorgeous summers.

This was our second home and we loved it. We continued on along the shaded path, dotted with warmth from the sun, the reality of what we were about to do, never far from our minds. I could feel the conviction in my spirit that it was "time" and although Kevin did too, I was impressed by his calm and peaceful demeanour. He was giving up so much. We all were! We considered the beauty of this place and all the years and painstaking effort it had taken to come this far in the music industry, including the connections and the friendships, the kids, their friends and activities. God was asking us to leave it all behind. We quickly shifted our thoughts to the here and now. We couldn't afford to reminisce too long. Our focus needed to be on the task at hand. We were being called away and that was that.

It was time to go! Kevin gave the final word that he'd be leaving his much coveted music gig at the hotel by the end of the week. We would be leaving the country the week after that! It was all absolutely surreal! Strangely, as only God can orchestrate these things, the day after he'd given "notice" I received a letter:

Dear Deborah,

Thank you for taking part in the telephone interview for the above post last week. I am sorry to have to tell you that we have now offered the post to another candidate who has accepted.

I had been unsuccessful in the job competition in Inverness. And we were moving our family to Inverness the next week! How exceptionally bizarre the timing was. If we had gotten the letter a day earlier, we might have seen it as a sign that we hadn't yet found the correct location. Given that we knew this move "wasn't about the job", Kevin had already given his notice, our belongings were already being shipped to Inverness and our van had been returned to those who'd originally gifted it, we were headlong into this thing, this move and this faith walk, big time!! Through it all though, I'll say it once again, we had a completely undeniable sense of peace.

In the natural, this move would have been completely insane but that's the beauty of the story. We weren't living according to the flesh. Admittedly, there were times when we'd catch ourselves focused on the things of this world. However, we noted that, whenever in this state, the peace of God seemed to slip away. We desperately wanted that peace in our lives and so we immediately self-corrected and got back onto the path of living according to the spirit. I was frequently reminded of when Peter walked on the water. When his eyes were fixed on Jesus, he was bold and confident, but when he looked down at his situation in the natural (water beneath his feet), he began to panic and sink. So, in the natural, we were leaving our home, work, family, friends and our country behind.

> We were on our way to Scotland, a place we'd never
> been, with three teenagers, and no home, no job,
> no friends, no family, no church, no ministry team,
> and no idea what God wanted us to do there.

Okay, that was in the natural. In the spiritual however, we really weren't any different than those in scripture who had left all, simply because it was required of them. "… And he went out not knowing where he was going. By faith he sojourned in the land of promise as in a foreign country …" (Hebrews 11:8-9).

At one point God had impressed upon my heart, by way of a picture, the choices before me, and how I might want to choose to handle the situation. In this image, it looked as though I was standing on an iceberg that was rocky with a definite, enlarging crack that was breaking apart and into two distinct pieces. I had one foot on each side. As they began to separate, it was becoming increasingly uncomfortable – almost to the place where I would be doing the splits. Because this skill is not in my repertoire of abilities, it would have been excruciatingly painful! God was showing me how I had one foot in the natural while the other was in the spiritual. Eventually, I needed to choose by moving one of my feet to join the other. That day I chose the spiritual and realized that life would never again be the same, a good thing because "it is the Spirit who gives life; the flesh profits nothing" John 6:63.

How Far is Too Far?

So what happens when you can't shake the feeling that a friend or acquaintance has taken their faith walk too far? How far is too far? Who determines where this invisible line might be and what it should look like? We know quite a few families who have a large number of children and for now, I'm reflecting on a conversation I'd had with a friend who has nine kids. We were discussing how funny it is that people tend to freely offer their opinions, usually without being asked and in some cases, without even being known. I was telling her how we had received criticism about, of all things, having had three of our children so close together.

I was completely mystified as to why others, especially strangers, would even care. This made me wonder about the comments a mother of nine would receive. She said, "You know, I'm not allowed to be tired. When I had one or two babies, it was not only okay that I be tired, it was expected." But as the number of children increased, the compassion toward her, decreased. Why is that? Why is it that two kids are OK, but nine is too many, or that a little faith is alright, but if you take it too far you're on your own?

> I am perplexed as to why when a person is called to a carry a heavy burden, others step away rather than stepping up.

Worse than this are the misguided comments and criticisms that ultimately make the load even heavier! At one point in my walk, I was maligned by a friend and church leader who maliciously pronounced, "What you call 'faith,' I call 'stupidity!'" Daggers pierced my heart, daggers thrown by a friend.

Over the ensuing weeks, he went on to boast to others about his witty repartee, turning a bad situation into a truly vicious attack. He had never witnessed faith in action and so his unfortunate response to seeing it live and in person was one of repulsion and disgust. Sometimes the resistance to faith isn't so blatant. There are occasions when despite having seen God move, people are resolute in their stance, digging in their heels, refusing to repent. In the end, though, we see from scripture that it is by faith and faith alone, that we will overcome. Living by faith pleases God and that's good enough for me.

> People desire a comfortable life. They are
> unable to come to terms with how a true walk
> of faith will fit their current lifestyle.
> Well ... simply put ... it won't!

Sowing and reaping in faith is also a difficult concept for many. In a culture that prides itself on "work," it is troubling for onlookers to come to terms with a walk of faith that God chooses to bless. When God blesses people based on His grace and their obedience and not on "works," it messes with people's minds. Right from the moment we committed to live for God, and without the benefits associated with being a formal pastor or missionary, we were frequently in a position of lack.

Most thought we should raise the white flag, lay down our swords, admit defeat, and call it a day, but we refused. We knew this was the road less travelled, and a narrow path leading to the eye of the needle and, therefore, difficult. We also knew we were wholly and wonderfully, directly in the centre of God's will for our lives.

> We had come to terms with the fact that our lives were no
> longer our own but that they belonged to Him.

Therefore, we needed to trust and believe for the miraculous. Again, those watching on had a difficult time assimilating what was happening especially *after* we started to receive those things for which we'd believed. They felt we needed to "work" for these blessings. What's funny, though, is that we were working! In fact, we were working very hard, but it was for the King of Kings and the Lord of Lords and not for a company, a business or a church. This was too difficult a concept for many to comprehend.

One example of this came during the concert days when, as I alluded to earlier, we desperately needed a replacement vehicle. Our poor, tired station wagon was nearing the end of its life so, for three years we prayed consistently, regularly, and specifically for a blue van. We were even planning, in faith, a trip across the country to visit Kevin's family, believing that God would provide us with a safe, large vehicle with which we could take this long overdue trip. Well, wouldn't you know it, about nine days before we were set to leave, we received news that the Lord had impressed upon someone's heart, to buy us a van of our choice!

When we got to the auto lot, chosen by God, there were two vans side by side, one blue and one green. The green one was not only newer but also in far better condition. We were stumped, trying to negotiate in our little itty bitty minds how this could be. We had prayed for a blue van. Then, as only God could ordain these things, our salesman, a Christian friend said, "Well, you can have the blue van that you prayed for or you can have something better that God picked out; it's your choice." We took the green van and never forgot those words. Interestingly, years later, we received a van on a long-term loan from friends, and it was blue!

When we received the green van, there were some who witnessed this rather extraordinary gift as too much to grasp while for others it was encouraging. Years later though, when God provided us with that home—the one we were blessed to "own" before leaving for Scotland—many who had been okay with us receiving the van were not okay with us receiving the home. Why is that?

> Why do we limit God? Why do we put a
> ceiling on what He can accomplish?

Why would grace begin and end with salvation? In fact, grace extends well beyond salvation.

Jesus' death and resurrection brought grace, it didn't stop grace.

Because of this inherent misunderstanding, it causes great unrest as to how and why our family has received such miracles. I don't think it's because we are any more special than the next person. I think it's simply because we believe in a great big God, for whom *nothing* is impossible! We believe He is who He says He is and that He'll do what He says He'll do. He keeps His word and so we do what's asked of us, knowing He will care for us. It's actually strange to me that people trust the government, their bosses and the companies they work for more than they trust God. If the company you work for says that they'll take care of you, why wouldn't the God of heaven and earth, who created you, do the same and more?

> God is in the business of miracles. We don't just believe for
> them … we rely on them.

All the members in our family have experienced physical healing. We have seen financial miracles, been blessed with a number of extravagant gifts and even lived through a few near death experiences. Here's the funny thing, though. Even with all this, there have been times when I've believed for the big things, but not the little things.

I was in my element and loving every opportunity that came my way to sing with my group of friends. We were scheduled to perform at a radio-thon and wouldn't you know it, I had laryngitis. I found myself somewhat resigned to this unfortunate fact and assumed we would work around it somehow.

The morning of the gig, I realized that I hadn't actually trusted God to heal my voice. So I prayed and asked for healing, that I might sing at the event. Although nothing seemed to have changed, in faith, I prepared and headed over to the event, still with no voice. I went up onto the platform and wouldn't you know it; He gave me my voice for the songs we were singing and then it was gone again! I learned a couple vital lessons as a result of this day. First, I realized I shouldn't only trust God for the big things but also the little things and, secondly, I should have believed for complete healing and not just for the event!

I choose to believe God can use us to reach entire communities or nations or even the whole world. Why should we only ask Him to give us five or six people to lead to Christ, when we could just as easily believe for hundreds, thousands or even millions? This isn't to focus on "numbers" but to shatter the limitations that we place on God. He's blessed me with the opportunity to see hundreds and hundreds of souls saved and I'm just an ordinary person with no formal Bible training. I hope to be a part of many more amazing moves of God. Think about who it is we're talking about – *God*, the one who created it *all*.

> Something tells me, He can handle our big prayers
> and that none of them are too massive for Him.

While I feel strongly about these and other dreams, I began to question the possibility that I had, perhaps, gone off the deep end. I needed to be reassured that I hadn't taken this faith thing "too far" as had been suggested. I wanted to know if visions and dreams as big as mine were as foolish as some thought, so I sought out godly counsel, the result of which was the following advice from a well-known pastor and author from the U.S. This is what he wrote to me:

First of all, God uses the person who has a dream, a vision, a goal. Nothing starts happening until somebody starts dreaming. Every accomplishment started off first as an idea in somebody's mind. If you aim at nothing, you are going to hit it.

Second, God uses the person who is willing to risk failure. When I moved here I had no money, no members, no building, and I didn't know a single person. We had literally moved on faith because God said, "Go." It was an enormous risk. We had no guarantee that we were going to succeed and there was no safety net beneath us. But God uses the person who is willing to risk failure.

Third, God uses the person who expects great things from God. You must be both realistic and optimistic. You must have high expectations. That is an evidence of faith. The difference between winners and losers is attitude. The person who says "I can," and the person who says "I can't" are both right. If you think you can't, believe me, you can't.

Finally, God uses the person who never gives up. God uses the person who is persistent, who is diligent, who doesn't know how to quit. The secret of success in the ministry is to just keep on keeping on. Outlast your critics. Great people are simply ordinary people who don't know how to quit. They don't know how to give up. Don't give up!

What a blessing and an encouragement this was, at a time when I had started to believe the sceptics. Thank God, for the wisdom of those who have gone before! This is precisely why we share our stories – to build one another's faith.

We only get to do this life once so, let's make it count!

Chapter 5

TROUBLE WITH FAITH

Trials and Tribulations

BECAUSE IT IS a less travelled road, the faith walk is frequently misunderstood. For this reason I'd like to address some of the stumbling blocks, barriers and misconceptions I've encountered over the years in the hopes of bringing clarity, understanding and even revelation to that which often mystifies and confounds. One of the most common, incorrect conclusions I've heard is that if the plan is of God and the one called is "on track" then everything will go smoothly.

> People mistakenly believe that if God is in it,
> the road will be easy and breezy. Although a
> lovely thought, it's not a biblical one.

Often these same people think that if the one called experiences difficulty then they have likely erred in some way. While this could be true for anyone at anytime, it's interesting to note that throughout scripture, those listening intently to God, who had been asked to do or say something as directed by the Lord, rarely made it to their destinations without experiencing trouble. The truth is that the Christian faith walk is not easy. So where does that leave us? Does this mean that trials and tribulations are a necessary part of the journey?

Well, in a word, "yes." I say this with some degree of trepidation, recognizing the fact that personal "religious" history will play a key role in how this response is viewed or understood. If you're one who's been indoctrinated with the belief that God is sitting up in heaven with a great big stick, just waiting for you to make a mistake so He can hit you with it, then it will be difficult for you to comprehend the breadth and depth of God's love for you and His gift of forgiveness through Jesus Christ. You may also struggle with seeing God as a Father who loves you unconditionally if you've had an earthly father who was a less than stellar human being.

If that is you, then this next section is not directed at you, but may still be of interest. The following thoughts are primarily intended for the consideration of those who are from backgrounds or churches that have simplified the Christian walk a little too much, having omitted the sections that deal with hardships.

I'm not trying to cause dissension in saying this, but neither of these extreme perspectives is fully correct. You can't talk about God and sin and not talk about God's mercy and grace. You also can't talk about faith and following Christ without talking about trials and tribulations that tend to come as part of the deal. Not long after I'd begun my walk of faith, I remember the comment of a friend who had been watching as I struggled with all the associated hardships, saying, "If this is what living by faith looks like, then why would anyone ever want to do it?" I was stumped!

> The truth is, that for most of us who have become so entangled by living "easy," a walk of faith that guarantees hardship, is not very appealing.

Strangely, though, there are places around the world and eras of time in which the very decision to give your life to Christ, to fully live for Him, pretty much means or meant, a death sentence. And not a simple death, but one of pain and torture. These people have a clear understanding of what it is to deny self, take up the cross, and lay down their lives for Christ. Let's consider this for a moment. Would you and I still choose Christ, if we knew this would be the result?

I am such a huge fan of the love of God, sharing the love of God, and experiencing the love of God but in truth, there is a side to the Christian walk that involves persecution and difficulties. I am concerned that in our zeal to see people saved (I have an evangelistic heart myself) we may have simplified the walk a little too much. I know that we can't feed solids to a baby but somehow even I, who had gone to church and small groups and Bible studies for most of my life, had missed this really important detail.

Perhaps it was my own fault in not seeking the truth as fully as I should have or maybe I was in denial that this part of the Word was as truthful as the love part. I really can't say for sure. However, one thing I can say for certain is that it's a pretty universal issue. Otherwise not only would I not have been so stunned by the harsh reality of what it took to stand with and for God but neither would the church folk around me have been so appalled. It was because they found the whole premise so unattractive and foreign to what they "knew" that they ultimately rejected this life and discarded me.

Paul encouraged the church to hang on to their faith through these trials. "No one should be shaken by these afflictions; for you yourselves know that we are appointed to this. For, in fact, we told you before when we were with you that we would suffer tribulations, just as it happened, and you know" (1 Thessalonians 3:3-4). Perhaps, when people in the church see someone moving outside the norm or even outside their own personal comfort zones, they allow worry, confusion or anger to take hold of them. They assume that if a person begins to have trouble, they must be either sinning or off track somehow.

Although this is possible, what I'm talking about here is the faith walk, the obedient walk, the walk that has you living for Christ. If people are never taught that in living for Jesus trouble will come, then it stands to reason they will react poorly when hardship hits someone they already view as having "gone astray." They assume the trouble these folks are experiencing is because they are in error. Not so! As a word of encouragement to those who've overcome in spite of these obstacles, God's Word clearly states that those who are persecuted for righteousness' sake *will* be blessed!

Trouble is usually part of the deal.

It may sound as though I've been picking on the church or the believers and I hope it doesn't, but here's why I'm saying what I'm saying. It's not to condemn but rather to encourage understanding. I hope that as a result of my sharing these experiences, others who choose this life, or whom God chooses for this life, will receive love and acceptance from within the body. You see, I fully expected to be persecuted by the world, but was completely unprepared for the persecution that came from within the church. Call me naive, but I really thought that believers would stand with me. Jesus said, "If the world hates you, you know that it hated me before it hated you and … A servant is not greater than his master. If they persecuted me, they will also persecute you." Here's the key, though …

Scripture speaks of persecution coming
from the world, not from the body.
If it comes from the body, then that is
on par with self-harming.

This is most assuredly not God's way. As I travelled down this road of discovery, bewildered by what I was encountering, I found that I would receive pockets of support, but more often than not I was patronized, disregarded, judged and in a number of cases, completely rejected by the body for living by faith. Why is that? I believe this happens because, as I said earlier, most aren't fully free of their "baggage."

This "stuff" that we've held onto can get very cumbersome, greatly hindering our progress and our ability to work together. Sometimes people are jockeying for position or perhaps lashing out due to insecurities or jealousy. There are other occasions when it's about a sin that's clouding a person's vision or simply because they don't like to see a faith walk that doesn't look like theirs. Whatever the reason, it's destructive and it slows a good work.

> Underlying or unresolved issues frequently seem to rear their
> ugly heads when attempting to work together for God.

Sometimes there can also be a nasty spirit that's found its way into a body of believers. This can also create problems. Obviously, it's not a good thing if there's resistance to the cause of Christ right *inside* the church. If we allow enemy strongholds into the church, we've obstructed both His blessings and our ability to effectively serve. I realize this isn't a popular notion, but the proof is in the fruit. If ugliness erupts from within the body then something evil has been given a "right." Why else would we "blindly" hurt one another? The blindness comes from somewhere and it certainly isn't God. I wonder if this is what Jesus meant when He said, "And a man's foes will be those of his own household."

> Satan already has the world where he wants it …
> let's not let give him the church too!

In humility, we need to bring our broken and fractured selves to Jesus for healing. We are all connected. We need one another. If we want to participate in the successful completion of God's plans, we need to be visibly different from the world. We must remain healthy in mind, body, soul and spirit so that we can fulfil our role … amicably. After all, a house divided against itself falls.

I thought people were supposed to know we are Christians by our love. What happened to that? We need to love one another even if we do things differently, see things differently or look a little different from one another. If we don't love, we have become more like the world than like God. I don't want to get dragged down by those who are quick to point out the splinter in my eye, completely unaware of the tree in their own, nor do I wish for the reverse to occur.

"A new commandment I give to you, that you love one
another: as I have loved you, that you also love one another."
—John 13:34

That's a pretty tall order! He doesn't infer or suggest, but actually commands us to love like He has. Notice the grammar; read
the words after the colon as one thought (as I have loved you, that
you also love one another). We must love as He has ... but Christ's
love for us is completely sacrificial, unconditional and absolutely
never *self*-serving. How can we ever measure up to that? Well, we
may not be able to, but He can, through us.

---

*Our youngest daughter exuberantly jumped into the van along with her
little buddy, talking a mile a minute about her upcoming birthday party
plans. I was parked outside the elementary school patiently waiting
for the rest of the crew to emerge when I overheard something being
said about an invitation having gone to a boy completely unbeknownst
to me. I felt a little exasperated since I had spoken with her ahead of
time about preparing her "invite" list prior to going to school so the
numbers wouldn't get out of control. I was keenly aware she was well
liked by many but our financial resources were limited. I decided to
wait and address it with her later, in private.*

*That evening I made another attempt to relate the guidelines for
the party.*

*"Honey," I began, "remember how we'd spoken about the number
of people you could invite to your party?"*

"Yes," she nodded.

*"Well, because you've already invited this boy, it means one of your
other close friends won't be able to attend."*

*I reminded her of our previous conversation and the agreed upon
number. She did recall and seemed to understand but the sadness in
her eyes broke my heart.*

"Why did you invite this boy?" I asked.

*"Well, Mommy," she began, "he isn't liked by anyone and he's
usually left out of things. He told me today that he has never been*

asked to a party before, no one has ever invited him so, I asked him because I wanted him to feel loved and included."

My heart was in my throat. It was apparent that my <u>little</u> girl had just taught me a <u>big</u> lesson. Needless to say, her party guest list grew.

Let's hope when our lives here on earth are over we have died to self, living as He commanded and enabled, loving and sharing one another's burdens as we walk together on the narrow path He has set before us. Until that happens we need to persevere through the barriers before us, refusing to allow criticism to discourage us or stop us from reaching our destiny, our calling. It can be a real kick in the gut when the cynics in our lives end up being the people or institutions we had admired.

Actually, it hurts, and it's disappointing but we need to shift that admiration over to God, with the understanding that He is the only one worthy of our praise and adoration. Although it can be painful, this shift towards dependency on God is a very good thing.

Misconceptions

I recognize that a big deterrent to living by faith is a fear of lack, of not having enough and having to rely on God who tends to operate in and through those around us. I really wish I didn't have to say this, but in all honesty, it *can* be part of the price to pay. It doesn't always need to be this way and it doesn't always remain this way, but it certainly *can* be a part of the equation and, I might add, not a very pleasant part. That is, until you gain a deeper, fuller understanding. I am only now beginning to grasp some of these concepts, so while there may be holes, I'd like to share what I've learned thus far.

Receiving help in whatever form or fashion is humbling. Even when we understand the concept that *everything* belongs to God, it is still difficult to acknowledge that there are occasions when we need to accept help from others. Why does "receiving" seem contrary to us? I think it's because we live in a culture that encourages and expects *self*-sufficiency. What's interesting to note is that this sort of independence, is in complete contradiction to how God operates.

> Jesus didn't do things independent of
> the Father or the Holy Spirit.
> Neither are we to act independently of Jesus.

Christ is the head and we are the body. We work together. If the head asks the arm and hand to pick something up and they don't, operations are slowed. If the foot moves, but without instruction from the head, or in cooperation with the ankle, it can prove disastrous. We work as a team. If the eyes see danger, but the body doesn't move to avoid it, then when ignored often enough, the eyes become weary of doing their job and the body gets battered. We are warned to not become weary while serving, for in due season we will reap!

When *self*-reliant, we are separated from the body. I think that sometimes the reason for lack is to ensure that those of us who may appear to be, or who actually are quite capable, would clearly know that we are *unable* to do anything *alone*, ahead of or separate from God's timing or plan! This is what happened, in part, to me. In order to avoid conflict and judgment I had become quite independent. This autonomy was partially about creating a protective "barrier" but it was also the result of incorrect teaching.

Society tells us we have the power within us to *have* or *do* anything we want, if we just put our minds to it. This is a worldly concept and not a godly one. In sharp contrast, God's Word says "I can do all things through Christ who strengthens me" (Philippians 4:13). It's through Christ, not in and of ourselves that we are able to do anything of lasting value. It's not about us or our self-created power! That is a lie of the enemy. It is all about God and His power. It's about the power of the Holy Spirit and the blood of Jesus; it's about the Trinity at work in and through us.

Even those who don't believe in God have received their gifts from Him. So, even if the unsaved don't use their talents to glorify God, scripture says these gifts are from Him and are irrevocable!

To move forward in faith, we must take our eyes off of ourselves and fix them on Jesus.

> It's *not* about God bringing glory to us.
> It's about us bringing glory to God.

God is a jealous God. He wants all the credit and all the glory; not just the parts we decide to offer back, but *all* of it. Often people see Him as a God of rules and regulations but He's a God of grace. That's why He sent His Son, Jesus. It was to obliterate law and legalism. He looks at the heart and desires that true and lasting transformation take place.

We can't earn His blessings by what we do or even by who we are but only by, and because of, Christ and His sacrifice. In our flesh, we sometimes like to revel in the spotlight but He loves us too much to permit that for long. He saves us from ourselves because if we take the glory, then we have turned our accomplishments into idols. Idols aren't just gold and silver statues, but they are anything that takes our focus off God and transfers it onto something else. This can even include that which we view as our own successes, possessions, careers or even our talents and it can happen to the most well-meaning individuals.

Picture the little old lady in the kitchen at church who becomes known for her cakes. In the beginning she is baking because she is gifted and wants to serve, but over time she finds herself seeking out and relishing the compliments of others, which begin to take a significant place in her heart, even to the point of giving her worth and "identity." By absorbing this identity, she begins to lose her true identity in Christ, thinking that it's the gift He gave her that gives her worth and position with God and man. But in actuality there isn't anything we can "do" to be made worthy. It's all about grace! God desires that we need Him and each other, in order that His will be done. In working as a team, He is assured all the glory. This is one reason that unity is vitally important and why Satan is out to destroy unity within the body.

We're all wired to give. What's fascinating though, is that the giving may look very different from one person to another. Some provide a listening ear while others offer sound advice. Some lead, others follow and although one might be called to "leave all" as led by God, another is called to finance that move.

It's teamwork. It's Kingdom work and it's God's way.
One role is no more significant than another.

I've also learned that the concept of giving-receiving-giving is an inescapable godly principle that's cyclical. We must give and we must receive. When we give, we are blessed with more to give and when we receive, we can bless the giver not only by graciously receiving but also by praying for them.

I have a theory that when we have received, we are given a really significant window of opportunity to pray blessings on the giver that will be far more effective than if prayed by anyone else. So when you receive, make sure you pray for the one who gave. Ask them about their needs, pray and then, God willing see their prayers answered through you! In the end, we've all worked together and everyone gets blessed. The book of Acts tells us, "Now the multitude of those who believed were of one heart and one soul; neither did anyone say that any of the things he possessed was his own, but they had all things in common … Nor was there anyone among them who lacked …" (Acts 4:32, 34).

Why then, with all this giving and receiving is there still lack?

I think it's because we're not fulfilling this strategy to its fullest and in the case of many an individual, not at all. Of course, there are also bigger problems at play with our governments, our economic systems and the ways in which our organized churches and charitable organizations are structured and how they distribute funds. Being self-reliant is somewhat rampant in our society and will take time to be reversed. I remember chatting with a dear, faithful friend about how, when you really sit back and look at western culture, a large portion of our lives is spent focused on growing our careers and accumulating "stuff". There's nothing wrong with stuff and there's nothing wrong with working hard and achieving success. It's simply that

> a walk of faith, be it for a season or forever,
> is simply *not* about *self*.

If it were about getting ahead, then much of what God has required of us and of others would be quite ludicrous, unwise and generally ridiculous. Quite to the contrary though, the great part of all of this is that it's about *Him*, the Great I AM, the King of Kings and the Lord of Lords. The focus is not on us and our accomplishments, rather it's on Him and His Kingdom work. The world tells us that dependency is equivalent to weakness. But truth be told, it takes strength and courage of conviction to put all our trust and faith in Him. He is God and we're not!

We should have no confidence in the flesh but only in Christ.

There's another misconception out there that says faith is for lazy people but faith isn't about slothfully sitting around, waiting for something to happen. Even those times when there's an expectation to rest in, or wait on the Lord, discipline and obedience in restraining oneself from rushing ahead of God, is necessary. It still requires prayer and remaining focused on the goal. I could be wrong in this, but I have a funny feeling that the people God curtails are often those with a propensity toward doing more than their part. It's the more sedentary individuals whom God may wish to encourage toward activity. The key point is that we are to do our part, no more, no less. This involves active listening, staying in the Word, seeking after and worshiping our Lord.

I think of faith as an action word.

Faith without works doesn't really amount to much. If I believe there is a God but choose not to follow Him then, as Scripture says, I'm really no different than the demons. Believing, in and of itself, doesn't require work for they (the demons) believe, but do not follow. It is in the "following" that we are active and our faith comes alive! Following requires actually doing something. Now there are also those who *do* many wonderful things and, although a blessing, this isn't faith either. We need faith *and* works. In order for faith to be alive, it must be acted upon. If I know that God wants me to bring His music to the world, but I don't actually do something as led, then it's been a rather empty or dead kind of faith.

In order for the walls of Jericho to fall down, God required that His people march around the wall for seven days before this would take place. They had to *do* something. "But be doers of the word, and not hearers only, deceiving yourselves" (James 1:22). We are told by Paul to press toward the goal, to strive for the faith of the gospel and to run the race before us. This, to me, sounds like something requiring effort. It doesn't seem passive and it certainly doesn't seem like a pursuit one could achieve in a zombie-like state but rather, the complete opposite. Pressing, striving and running sound like action words. They even sound like work! Work like this requires a keen mind, energy and passion.

Throughout the three years we brought music to the prison, we not only needed to be prepared musically, but there was quite a rigorous logistical procedure involved, including background inspections, criminal record checks and orientation sessions. It was necessary for every volunteer at the prison to do this. When a member of our team was unable to attend, even just once, this meant the replacement would need to go through the entire process, which could take up to six weeks.

It was a race against time for each of our team members to get from their own church service and over to the prison on time. Sound gear, instruments, music stands and more all needed to be loaded in and out of vehicles, onto dollies and then, through a number of secured doors. All of this took place before we'd even gotten to the room where the service would be held.

Once there, we still needed to set everything up, sound check and pray. Yes, it was like a church plant, only different. It was different because most of our team members had already done this once that day at their own services, and now they were doing it again. It was also unique because of all the security measures and doors at the prison. We could only pass through one door at a time so it was a lengthy process. I was blessed with a truly dedicated and passionate group. Although it was a cumbersome task and a hefty commitment, there was no groaning, no complaining, only loyalty and faithfulness.

Serving and following are choices and they require effort.

Jesus did *not* say, "Join me. Life will be easy as we kick up our heels and then relax with a fruit drink on the beach." He said, "Whoever desires to come after me, let him deny himself and take up his cross and follow me" (Luke 9:23). Oftentimes this means not going with the flow, not fitting in with the mainstream, and maybe even for a time not having nice things. Ouch!! If that doesn't sound overly appealing to you, well, it didn't to me either.

What others don't realize about us "crazies" is that the choice wasn't to have trouble, create hardship for ourselves, upset our friends, or anything of the sort. That wasn't the choice we made but rather a by-product associated with the commitment to deny ourselves and live for Christ. Although folks may fear for our sanity, I must assure and reassure them that we are quite lucid, certain, passionate, convinced and convicted about that which we've been called to and what we'd love from those around us, is prayer and whatever support they are led to offer.

From what I have read in the Bible, usually when Jesus forgave, healed or delivered someone, it was as a result of *their* effort in seeking Him out and *His* grace and love poured out upon them. He asks us to seek and to knock. He requires that we give and serve, worship and pray.

We need to activate our faith by stepping into it,
not by expecting it to suddenly come upon us.

99

A faith that is pure of heart sees us visiting orphans and widows who are troubled. These are activities that require effort. And yet, while we must be active, we are not justified by these works. We shouldn't expect our actions or good works to bring us into right relationship, as that would be based on law. We are justified solely by grace. Bottom line though, a God-inspired "work" *will* activate our faith.

> "For as the body without the spirit is dead,
> so faith without works is dead also."
> —James 2:26

Calling

I would encourage you to seek the Lord in all things and at all times, expectant that He will hear your prayers and respond. Personally, I'd rather not rely on friends or leaders to provide me with answers, guidance and revelation. While godly advisors are a blessing, I would prefer to go directly to the throne room of God.

> "Let us come boldly to the throne of grace, that we may obtain
> mercy and find grace to help in time of need."
> —Hebrews 4:16

I believe that Jesus is my Lord and Saviour and I need only follow Him. Yes, I should honour those in authority here on earth, knowing that their authority is given them by God, but first and foremost, I must follow, serve and receive direction from the Lord Himself. I believe there's a faulty teaching out there that says we will receive inspiration and instruction primarily through godly leaders *rather than* directly from God. Now, if we are referring to proven prophets who actually have a word from the Lord that rings true in our spirits, that is one thing, but what I'm referring to is something very different.

It would seem that, over the years, priests and pastors have been elevated to a position that is not entirely scriptural. As a result of this "promotion," they have become our "connection" to God. While the hearts of these men and women of God are typically pure, with a sincere desire to assist their flock in better hearing and knowing God, what seems to have occurred over time is unhealthy because we have asked them to perceive what the Lord is saying on our behalf rather than learning to hear from God ourselves. I don't wish to undermine these faithful servants who have committed their lives to shepherding the sheep but rather to encourage the rest of us to broaden our perspectives and grow in the knowledge that we too have Kingdom authority.

It saddens me to think of the number of people who have missed out on executing a directive from God because it wasn't provided by, or confirmed through a church leader. In giving others the power to determine our worthiness, our calling, or to give us purpose and direction, we have both esteemed man and devalued God. I know that sounds harsh, but in truth, these leaders won't be with us on judgment day. We will stand alone before the Lord. In Galatians 1:10, Paul says "... if I still pleased men, I would not be a servant of Christ."

Knowing God in a uniquely intimate and personal way is the primary manner by which our faith grows. As we grow in relationship with Him, an unshakeable peace, revelation and power of conviction comes into our hearts, based on that which we *know* to be true. Nothing beats having a certainty based on first-hand knowledge, wisdom and assurance. After all Jesus said,

"My sheep hear My voice, and I know
them, and they follow Me."
—John 10:27

God has frequently and historically, asked people to do things that don't "fit" within the framework of a pre-existing structure, programme or the mandate of an existing organization. Again, our Christian culture can limit us when it dictates that whatever God requires of us must line up with an already established umbrella, organization or banner under which it be "covered," ordained or blessed.

Under what banner were the disciples?
Under what umbrella was Moses?
How does the call on Esther's life fit with this theory?
These people were under the banner of the Lord!

101

I'm not against being under a godly organization and I also believe that prayer support and accountability in ministry is vital. However, God is doing a new thing and therefore the old wine skin or the old ways simply won't work. If we dig in our heels and maintain the expectation that each call or work must match up with something already deemed as worthy, then we are in for a big surprise.

This mind-set is hugely restrictive. It took me a long while and a major paradigm shift to look at this with new eyes, but once I did, this deep and undeniable revelation brought incredible peace and freedom! How wonderful it is to know that I am fully, completely and directly under the great I Am.

This shift in thought may take some time to process, so for now, try to think of it in this way. If we as parents, instruct our children to wash the dishes, then we expect they will comply and follow the task through to its completion. It would be laughable for that child to later approach another of your children, asking for a second opinion, especially when they have already heard from you, the highest authority on that issue. Although this may sound silly, the concept isn't. I think God must shake His head in bewilderment each time we question the "validity" of His request by checking it with another person. We may *say* that we don't trust man above God, but our actions can prove otherwise.

I realize we likely do this because we have been conditioned to trust that others hear God better than we do, however, as long as the request lines up with scripture, a second opinion is really not required. Confirmation is a very good thing, but I've found the most effective confirmation usually comes via a vessel chosen by God, not a perspective or person selected by us.

Having come to this revolutionary understanding, I then made another startling discovery that complicates matters even further. I came to the realization that some pastors were never actually "called" to be pastors. Now before jumping to a position of defence, allow me the opportunity to explain what I mean by this. What I believe may have happened is that, over time, when one felt "called" into ministry, they were funnelled into the role of pastor/priest or missionary. The position of a minister is, generally speaking, the most "secure" and the most conventional, while that of the missionary is familiar but requires more effort and provides less stability. Here's what I'm wondering …

> Where is the place, the job or the support
> for the prophet, the apostle,
> the teacher or the evangelist if they don't
> choose to become a pastor?

How many of those who are anointed in these areas slid into the role of pastor out of necessity? It's understandable if this was the only outlet for ministry, "work" or a job. Again though, this would mean that many of those currently in the role of "pastor" were never actually meant to be pastors. Our culture has structured "the church" in such a way that most of the funding is based around the role of "pastor," a position mentioned only a couple of times in all of Scripture. Appropriate allowance has not been afforded the other roles. Not only that, but pastors are expected to fulfil a number of obligations that are likely well outside their gifting, calling and anointing.

Conversely, there are others who have remained confident in their callings, convinced God was asking them to assume the role of prophet, apostle, evangelist or teacher, but because they didn't "fit" within the existing parameters, nor did they feel led to the local church, inevitably had nowhere to go. Many of these felt unable to carry out the call on their lives. How sad!

What this means is that we have a number of discouraged pastors who were never called to be pastors but have been charged with a role they aren't equipped to fill. We have frustrated prophets, apostles, evangelists and teachers who have not fulfilled their callings because there has been no place for them, causing them to move into unsuitable positions. And finally, there is one more group. These are the prophets, apostles, evangelists and teachers who did not become pastors, but against all odds and regardless of the cost, chose to be obedient to the call on their lives regardless of this fact.

This group receives virtually no support, walking exclusively by faith, with no regular income, dodging "religious" bullets and persecution, and seeking to do that which has been asked of them in a world and a church culture that doesn't recognize them or their calling. Often they are chastised by the mainstream church and called "lone rangers" who have lost their way. I have an affinity to this final group and am blessed to know that I am in good company.

> Even Jesus was seldom acknowledged as the Saviour, healer, redeemer and king that He was, and is, because of people's preconceived notions of how a king should look or act.

Jesus didn't present Himself as royalty and man often didn't recognize His authority but that doesn't change the fact that He was and is the King of Kings and the Lord of Lords. He simply walked in and with an authority given Him by His Father, all the while being a servant to all. He knew His call and His destiny and He fulfilled His mandate. In God's realm, the last is first and the first, last.

To be great in God's kingdom, we must serve. To gain life, we must lose it. His ways are not ours. It's all flipped upside down! As one who is committed to a life of faith, I desire to be true to the call on my life, even if it means going against the norm.

For those who hurl accusations, presuming that this group sees itself as "better," I am aghast. I cannot imagine seeing myself as being above anyone. The very thought that one person would see themselves as more valuable than another is a very scary slippery slope! I don't think it would take God long to shut this down with a few sharp reminders of what it took to get us to where we are. I think He'd cause us to recall the fiery furnace of trials and testing that He used to refine us and bring us to a place of complete surrender. And how, once in this broken, helpless, contrite state, He was at long last able to begin to use us for His purposes.

I actually went through a time of suffering that left me feeling so completely beaten down that it was almost to the place of paralysis. While in this mind-set, I came very close to losing my identity in Christ. This is also not a good place to be. When we feel that badly about ourselves, it can become a huge stumbling block to God being able to use us. Satan will hang on tight to self-hatred and will feed it with all things unhealthy. While dying to self is a prerequisite to the faith, we should balance this off by knowing who we are in Christ and who Christ is in us.

> We need to remain steadfast knowing we are sanctified, redeemed and bought with an incredible price.

We ought to be filled with the truth of how God sees us, assured that even when we are in error, He loves us. When we are remorseful and repentant, requesting God's forgiveness through His Son, Jesus, not only does He forgive us, but He wipes the slate clean. He has no memory of our sin. Satan, however, has a very long and evil memory. It is he who wants to ensure that we not forget our mistakes. When we are wrapped up in guilt, despair and self-condemnation, we are of little use to God, and that's just how Satan likes it! Don't allow Satan's lies to infiltrate your mind or your spirit.

We need to grab hold of the freedom that's ours in Christ! It's meant for all of us, not just some of us. When living for Him, we are *all* chosen, adopted, joint heirs with Christ, justified, righteous, sanctified, redeemed, accepted, healed, and deeply loved which makes us *all* His favourites! Galatians 2 says, "God shows personal favouritism to no man ..."

Whenever possible, speak out the truths of God and don't receive the lies of the enemy. Let's continually remind ourselves of who we are and who it is we serve. Our roles have no bearing on how deeply He loves us. Just because one child is asked to take out the trash and the other to set the table, doesn't put one above the other. Again, we are the body of Christ, and each part is integral and important. An ear cannot be an eye and shouldn't try.

> Those called to a task with heavy responsibility are usually humbled and feel ill-equipped to serve in their callings.

Regardless of how inadequate one feels, obedience is expected. I've noticed that those who observe our walk tend to focus on either the highs—the cool moves of God, the miracles, the "wow!"

factor—or the lows, moving against the "flow," experiencing hardship and the minimalistic lifestyle. Being an optimist, I would likely tend toward concentrating on the good elements myself, but the truth is, that both exist. In order to experience and see God in a heightened form also determines that there will be, like it or not, sacrifice, pain and suffering involved. In our flesh, we only want the highs.

> He gives us a choice as to whether or not
> we will drink of the cup given us.

Even Jesus struggled when He begged of the Father, prior to his crucifixion, "if it is possible, let this cup pass from Me." Of course, He also said, "Nevertheless, not as I will, but as You will." Although, none of us desire the difficult days, they are part of the journey. No one grows on the mountaintop. It's in the valley and as a result of "the climb" that we are stretched and bettered.

Life on the Edge

Our final week in Canada was upon us. It was strange to think we were leaving our home and native land behind. We were confident we'd be back to visit, but had no idea as to whether or not we'd ever live in Canada again. It was bittersweet. Before we knew it, we were packed; five people, fifteen pieces of luggage, passports and visas in hand, all set for our adventure, armed with little more than our Bibles, God's promises and the prayers of those who were standing with us! We were blessed to spend time with my parents at the airport prior to leaving the country. It was wonderful to see them and to know that they were blessing us as we went.

As I embraced my mom and dad at the gate, I could see the tremendous look of pride on their faces. They had always been incredibly supportive and this time was no different.

Today, though, I saw something particularly touching in my Dad's eyes. It was an immense sadness coupled with an undeniable love for

*his family. He looked at us with those warm blue eyes as his only
daughter, her husband, and these three beloved grandchildren were
about to embark on yet another phase of this journey with God. He
was proud but also heartbroken to see us go and bore the countenance
of a man who clearly thought he'd never see us again.*

*I tried to remain positive, wrestling with my emotions, all the
while attempting to stay focused on the mission at hand. And so, with
smiles on our faces and clouded vision, we hugged as they blessed
us and bravely wished us well. We waved, blew kisses and walked
through the gate.*

To say that it was easy to leave everything and everyone we
knew behind would be untruthful. Essentially, our entire history,
both the good and the bad, was being left in this land while our
future, a complete mystery to us, was before us in a new country.
Though difficult to comprehend, we were greatly encouraged by
Jesus' words:

> "Assuredly, I say to you, there is no one who has left house
> or parents or brothers or wife or children for the sake of the
> kingdom of God who shall not receive many times more in
> this present time and in the age to come everlasting life."
> —Luke 18:29, 30

This verse provided us with a sense of hope and expectation as
we ventured out into the unknown. I realize that speaking of the
"unknown" in this way must sound more like a line from a Star
Trek episode than a truthful word spoken by a person of faith, but
however you'd like to view it, we were stepping into uncharted
territory. "For we walk by faith, not by sight" (2 Cor. 5:7). To walk
by faith we must be willing to undertake that which is unfamiliar,
trusting that God is not only leading us but is also holding us by
the hand, gently and purposefully guiding us every step of the way.

My personal faith walk seems to have changed and progressed
over time and while it's not something "typical" or predictable, it
is also not something particularly puzzling either. I touched on

this earlier, but what I found fascinating about the process God took us through in preparation for our time in Scotland was the consistency in how He spoke and in what He expected. I'll reiterate. He would provide a word like "get passports" or "get luggage" or whatever it happened to be. We would do as told and only after we had obeyed, would we receive confirmation.

When we purchased our luggage, as directed, we discovered that it was the last day of a sale in a town that had very few options in the way of department stores. If we hadn't obeyed at the time that He'd spoken, we still would have gotten the luggage but the cost would have been significantly more and our options would have been limited. In the case of the passports, we were unable to be instantly obedient because of a very real barrier, a lack of funds. So, we committed it to prayer and He provided within twenty-four hours. This allowed us the means to move forward, which we did, without delay.

Confirmations *only* came *after* we had been obedient. Even in the case of making the decision to ship our belongings to Inverness, it was only *after* we had called the shipping company and committed to the destination, that the confirmation of the location came. Again, it was imperative that we hear, act in obedience and then we would receive confirmation.

> Early in our walk, we would have required a number of confirmations prior to stepping out to do anything, but as time passed, this all changed.

Not only did the confirmations *not* come until after we had obeyed, but more often than not, we were also given *no* further instructions until we had done what had been asked of us. We needed to trust that we could "hear" and He needed to trust that we would obey. So much of what I see in the Christian community is contrary to faith. I hear people say things like, "God said I'm to leave my job right away, but I'm not going to do that until I have something else." If my husband and I had used that logic, and it is logical, then we wouldn't have experienced Scotland because, in the end, as you will soon discover, there never was a "job" in the worldly sense.

Those who view our actions in the natural, say that these decisions make us reckless and unwise. To be honest, in the natural, it does appear fairly irresponsible, but when looking at it through spiritual eyes, it's not.

What's the difference between living by faith and being reckless? Were the disciples too hasty when they dropped everything to follow Jesus? What about Jonah? He hesitated, ran in the opposite direction, causing hardship and delay. God gave Jonah an opportunity to repent whereas Lot's wife disobeyed and, within the blink of an eye, became a pillar of salt. I'd rather not test God's patience any more than I already have.

> If I've made a commitment to follow God,
> then I'm going to follow God.

It's not about how good it feels or how comfortable it is or how it looks to others but it's about fully embracing the Christian walk of faith, because that's what's required of me! I've often heard people say that God won't give us more than we can handle. This is *not* true. Of course He will! He gives us more than we can handle, so that we will draw closer to Him and He can handle it for us. This way, He receives the glory. The Scripture that is frequently misquoted is from 1 Corinthians 10:13, which is in reference to "temptation," not hardships! Bottom line, He is worthy of our praise and we can trust Him. There are lots of ups and downs but it's tremendously exhilarating to walk hand-in-Hand with the King.

Chapter 6

FAITH THAT OVERCOMES

Pressed, not Crushed

IN TELLING THIS part of the adventure, I wish I could report a journey of smooth sailing but alas, what we experienced was more accurately, a rocky and stormy ordeal! Somehow, we wrongly assumed that because preparations in Canada had been so easy (a high), that the entire process would be effortless – *not*! This is when the reality of it being God's plan and not ours was clearly evident. Upon our arrival in Scotland, we were confronted with a substantial "low," as we faced the bleak and startling reality that there was absolutely *nothing*, from a worldly perspective, in place. There was no one to greet us. There was no one to show us around. There was no one to help us get oriented. There was no one to teach us the Scottish ways.

We were completely and totally at the mercy of God.

Obviously this is *not* a bad place to be, but trusting God at such a deep level from such a seemingly helpless state of being, was beyond uncomfortable. We encountered a number of challenges right from the get go. Once we'd collected our belongings, we needed to find a vehicle to transport us to the Bed and Breakfast.

Given that automobiles are smaller in the U.K. (I guess most people only have one or two children), this dilemma turned out to be an ongoing obstacle throughout our entire time in Scotland. However, on this particular day, we not only needed to move five people, but also a *lot* of luggage.

Once we'd sorted out the transportation challenges we discovered that because the houses are also smaller than what we were accustomed to, there wasn't even enough room for all our suitcases at the "B & B." We were also stunned to discover the B & B didn't have any Internet connection, nor did it have a telephone! Everything was different, from driving on the opposite side of the road, to terminology, to systems and technology, to absolutely everything. We'd only just arrived and were already experiencing more of a culture shock than anticipated. At least we spoke the same language, sort of!

> We barely understood a word they said but that was,
> apparently, part of the fun!

The first few days in Inverness were challenging and stressful and the task before us, daunting. It was difficult to find a frame of reference, because everything was so different. We needed to find a neighbourhood in which to live, a home, a school, jobs, a bank, a place of worship and more. We were overwhelmed.

Our "home base" turned out to be of no real use to us because the B & B where we were "staying" was locked up throughout the day. This meant the five of us meandered (mostly on foot) throughout the city for hours at a time, each and every day for fourteen days.

The first thing we noticed on these ridiculously long days was the incredible spiritual oppression. It was thick. This is the only way that I can describe the experience or sensation. From the very first day that we began to orient ourselves in the town centre, we absolutely knew that we needed to be outfitted in our spiritual armour and immediately began to pray for the city and the country, believing that God's desire was to heal and bless this land. We boldly asked that with every step we took, God would break off that which bound many of these people in a somewhat depressive state, something I'll speak more about later.

We decided to launch our Scottish adventure by searching for a good school. It made sense that our first stop be the school board. Unfortunately, this was of no help. What we did learn was that not only were our kids later to start than anticipated, but that many of the schools were already full and did not accept new students. We enquired as to which schools did have availability only to be told that it was our responsibility to find out for ourselves! This meant we needed to call or visit each institution to see if they would accept our kids. In a daze, the five of us set out once again, wandering the city streets, investigating schools, without a vehicle, a phone, or a computer.

> This lack of "customer service" was just one of the many occasions in which we were reminded that we were no longer in Kansas ... I mean ... Canada!

The only redeeming aspect associated with all this running around, was the fact that we were familiarizing ourselves with the city! There didn't appear to be any internet cafes and so we were ecstatic when we stumbled upon some computers at the library. Whew! While they limited our time on them, at least we were able to let our friends and family know that we were safe.

In a valiant attempt to use our "allotment" of computer time wisely, we also tried to investigate the Inverness housing situation. We were shocked to find that rentals were double the price we had paid in Canada *and* one also had to pay council taxes *and* these very same houses were less than half the size! We also learned one could not rent a home without having a bank account.

Armed with that crucial piece of information, we headed off to the bank to get an account. This is where things went from bad went to worse. They informed us that one cannot get a bank account without an address! What?? To reiterate,

> we couldn't get a house without a job or a bank account and we couldn't get a bank account without an address!

113

On top of all that, the banks wouldn't take our traveller's cheques. We had no credit cards and were faced with the distressing news that the Canadian dollar was at a value of less than half the British pound. In essence, with one swift move, we had just lost more than half our money and we didn't have a lot to begin with!

This is more significant than it sounds because the ramifications of this discovery were that rather than the anticipated six months to get settled, we could only afford three! After that, we would have no money! It was becoming next to impossible to find a silver lining. We decided to look for jobs. This would require getting a National Insurance Number (similar to a SIN or a SSN). After setting out to do this, we were told that we needed to prove that we had applied for jobs *before* they would give us the card. Strangely, we were unable to fill out on-line job applications without a NIN! Again, to clarify,

> we needed a National Insurance Number in order to apply for a job but we couldn't apply for work without a National Insurance Number!

Yes, we were shaking our heads too! I'd never heard of anything so absurd. It was discouraging beyond words and I felt as though I had entered the twilight zone. We had no choice but to keep moving. If we had believed the "theology" that if God was in it, all would go smoothly this would have been a mistake of gargantuan proportions.

After fourteen gruelling hours of walking from one school to another, to housing offices and potential "lets" (rental property locations) along with a number of other stops along the way, I looked over at my kids, astounded. This was day three and they hadn't complained ... at all! Personally, I could feel myself losing a grip on what little remained of my positive attitude and yet here were my kids – all of whom were at an age and stage when this entire experience could have been viewed as disastrous and they were persevering through the trials like real troopers.

Gratitude swelled up inside of me and the tears were difficult to contain. I could feel tremendous pressure on my chest as the burden before us seemed insurmountable. Had we made a mistake? Was it supposed to be this difficult? I was desperate to understand and fraught with discouragement. It was the steady and unwavering attitude of my teens that motivated me and strengthened my resolve to carry on.

When we next accessed a computer, I received an email that shattered my heart. It carried with it the news that my Dad had been diagnosed with Metastatic Amelanotic Melanoma. Cancer. We were stunned, disheartened and growing increasingly weary of the obstacles before us and the effort it was taking to disallow depression and heartache from overtaking us. We were absolutely in a "low" having found ourselves not simply on the mission field, something we were somewhat prepared to face, but also on the battlefield with very few reinforcements and not a lot of arsenal at our disposal. To be honest, those initial days felt like a nightmare. The battle was on!

Victory in Battle

Although I've mentioned the challenges associated with spiritual warfare, I haven't really delved into it much, mostly because this is both a sensitive and a very big subject. However, I would be remiss if I didn't address the reality of what it is to operate while under serious opposition.

The fact is, we Christians do indeed have an enemy and his name is Satan. While we serve a God who wants to save us, set us free, love us, forgive us and provide us with everlasting life, the enemy wants nothing more than to discourage us, defeat us, divide us and destroy us. If we wander out onto the battlefield completely unaware, then we are on dangerous ground.

Initially, when producing the concerts, I had unwittingly moved into the enemy camp, quite unaware of the ramifications of having performed such an act. While it's right and good to go into the world, remember that just as soldiers don't go to war without a strategy and an understanding of their enemy, neither should we.

So, when you go, be prepared!
Warfare is a very real part of the faith journey.

When Christians keep to themselves, they aren't a very significant threat to the enemy and yet Satan is still known to instigate strife and division whenever possible. However, the heat really gets turned up when we, with Christ in us, infiltrate the world, a place Satan sees as his territory. It's at this point that the enemy is incredulous at the apparent "audacity" of our actions, motivating him to pull out all the stops in an attempt to prevent further godly activity. We needn't allow ourselves to be scared off by this, but we also shouldn't diminish the reality of the situation.

"Be sober, be vigilant; because your adversary the devil walks about like a roaring lion seeking whom he may devour."
—1 Peter 5:8

What's interesting to note here, is that this Scripture says "may" devour. Satan needs our permission to do this. If we stand fast, well-equipped with knowledge and understanding, confident that we live in victory with Christ whose very name causes the enemy to quiver in fear and flee, we'll know the security and peace that we have in Him. That's incredibly good news! We are instructed to submit to God, resist the devil and then live with the assurance that he will leave us alone. We as believers have authority, in Jesus' name, over the devil. Jesus, who reigns in us, is far more powerful than the enemy. Once we recognize our delegated authority and effectively use that authority, we will be in a very good position to go into battle. The following verse is critical to understanding that authority.

"Behold I give you the authority to trample on serpents and scorpions and over all the power of the enemy, and nothing shall by any means hurt you."
—Luke 10:19

That is powerful! It says that "nothing" will hurt us! How comforting to know that even in the midst of trials, the battle has already been won. We who are in Christ are on the winning team. We've been given a sneak peek at the scoreboard and we win hands down!

Throughout our years in the Canadian Rockies, most of our time was spent in a provincial park where wildlife was free to roam. We were accustomed to this and so I felt comfortable going for walks on my own through wooded areas.

On one such trek, I was deep in thought when the Holy Spirit prompted me to make some noise by clapping my hands. As I did this, I came around the bend only to see that I had startled, just a few feet in front of me, a bear ... a large bear. In fact, it was a full-grown grizzly. We were used to being surrounded by elk, deer, the occasional moose and a number of black bears but never before had we encountered a grizzly. Although my heart skipped a beat, I was remarkably calm.

Slowly backing away, I remembered what I'd learned from a documentary, which was to talk and wave my arms as a signal to this poorly sighted animal that I was a person and not a predator. As I was doing this, I realized that the words I had spoken were words of spiritual authority: "I have dominion over you, in Jesus' name, and you don't want me!" The bear went his way and I went mine. Well actually, I went in the opposite direction. I have faith but I'm not crazy!!

> I'm convinced that there are many occasions when trouble
> comes and all we need to do is take authority.

Prior to one of the concerts, we were having some fairly significant issues with the theatre's high-end sound gear. None of the professional technicians could sort out the problem. Frustrated, they decided it might be a blown fuse. Moments after I left the theatre to find a replacement fuse, I prayed a prayer of authority, binding the enemy from touching the gear. Almost immediately after praying, my cell phone rang. It was the technicians advising me

I could return because the gear was, "for some unknown reason," working again!

Another example was the day we were setting up for our outdoor gospel music festival. One of the members of our team was made aware of a woman, unknown to us, who was making her way around the grounds. As it turned out, she was a witch who was there on a mission of her own. She was as determined as we to see change, however with a very different outcome in mind. We gathered together and prayed with the victory that we knew was ours until she left. In the spirit, one member who wasn't on site at the time had "seen" her leave something behind. He told us not to worry, that God was going to deal with it Himself. So, having done our part, we left Him to do His.

At the event the following day, there were so many miraculous activities that I had completely forgotten about the witch from the day prior. What's fascinating is that God hadn't forgotten His promise and while our group was worshiping on the stage, He took care of what the witch had left. It was a very hot day with absolutely no breeze until the moment that a focused heavenly wind passed directly over the stage and through our banner, which was attached to the roof of the stage. The wind blew from one end to the other and over to a place on the ground beside the stage where these white wings, for want of a better word, touched down and then lifted again from the very place where the witch had left her little "gift." The Lord used what was intended for evil to bless us! Of course, the crowd that was gathered gasped with awe and reverence.

"... thanks be to God, who gives us the victory
through our Lord Jesus Christ."
(1 Corinthians 15:5)

We are given a strategy as to how to handle ourselves in the battle and there are lots of good books on this subject that I would encourage you to read, but for now, at the very least, be certain to put on your armour each and every day as outlined in Ephesians 6:11-17: "Put on the whole armour of God, that you may be able to stand against the wiles of the devil." Alert the heavenlies aloud each and every day, as to who it is that you serve. Let there be no doubt that you are under the power, authority and jurisdiction of Jesus Christ.

It is here that I would like to share a truly freeing perspective that I hope will encourage you as it did me. A friend of mine was preaching one day and spoke about not only knowing one's enemy but also how crucial it is to know one's own army! I thought this was very insightful. While there are Christians who don't want to acknowledge that the devil exists, there are others who are more familiar with demons than they are with angels. I find this to be rather peculiar.

Scripture clearly indicates that both demons and angels exist.

In having a deeper understanding of the army that stands with us and for us, our fortitude to walk in faith is strengthened. I would encourage you to gain a greater understanding of the spiritual realm, or that which is supernatural. This isn't new fangled mumbo jumbo jargon. This is scriptural.

Many people in the Bible received visitations from angels. We are told that in end times, God will pour out His spirit on all flesh. Dreams and visions will occur more frequently and, I might add, they already are, which means exactly what it sounds like it means! Time is short. The supernatural realm of heaven is merging with the natural as His Kingdom comes to earth. This is why, with each passing day, there is more talk of the supernatural in the world and in the church. Ask God for wisdom in this so that you might easily discern the work of the enemy from the work of the Lord.

If you've hit a formidable wall in your battle and nothing seems to be able to knock that thing down, then keep in mind that it may not have been put there by Satan. God is also known to create barriers, but they are constructed for good, to teach us something or to preserve His timing.

If you take authority and it doesn't seem to be "working," either persevere, covet the prayers and assistance of friends and spiritual leaders, fast, or when all else fails, trust that it's God's will, God's "wall" and it's in His hands. The Lord is sovereign. He will create calamity and harden hearts to suit His plans and purposes. There's no real formula for "knowing" if it's Him or not, other than knowing Him, growing in the Spirit, in the Word and in prayer.

We all need to work through those times when we are unsure and determine whether we are to wait on the Lord or push through the difficulty. Pray that your eyes and ears be opened to the leading of the Holy Spirit. Remember, too, that if faith is like a muscle, then the best and only way to grow that muscle is by battling through the resistance.

Without resistance or trouble, our faith would never grow!

Pushing Through

During those initial days in Scotland, I felt despondent and be-leaguered. One evening as I sat on our bed at the B & B, re-hashing the situation in my mind, our son unexpectedly appeared at the door, Bible in hand. Being a quiet, introspective and unassuming young man, it was remarkable to me that he had wilfully come to us with both Scripture and insight. I think I was as stunned as I was encouraged, by the obvious growth. His words and heart inspired me to carry on, despite the oppression that threatened to consume me. Although there were many more obstacles with which to deal, and a multitude of emotions to control (too many to list) we kept on plodding through the muck and mire.

I did decide to email a trusted friend, coveting her prayers, knowing that we were absolutely in need of break-through. She had a dream that very night in which we were all surrounded by some very frightening tornadoes! She instinctively knew the meaning behind the dream. Our family had arrived in this country, purposefully, rightfully, with ancestral ties and in accordance with God's wishes and the enemy was not happy. This had apparently kicked up some serious spiritual dust, dust of tornado-sized proportions! So with that, my dear friend enlisted others to pray and fast with her.

"… for assuredly, I say to you, if you have faith as a
mustard seed, you will say to this mountain, 'Move
from here to there', and it will move and nothing
will be impossible for you. However, this kind does
not go out except by prayer and fasting."
—Matthew 17:20-21

I am delighted to say that it was soon after their act of obedience,
that mountains began to move! The Lord led us to the district of
Culloden/West Hill and it was here, in this very region that we
finally, at long last found a great school and miraculously, still
without a bank account, we found our home. Break-through! We
were elated and deeply grateful.

---

*"The only way to secure a rental home without a bank account would
be to deal directly with the home owner." This was the firm response
from the letting agency. With that piece of information, our options
had dwindled substantially. The house we were about to go and see,
like the majority of homes we'd found, was in the hands of a solicitor.
Kevin and I seriously doubted whether it was worth the time and cab
fare to go and take a look.*

*As we discussed the possibility of not making the trip, our son
piped up with, 'I think we should go and see the house, because you
never know what God might do!' We were stunned by both his faith
and his wisdom. We agreed, ordered a cab and off we went. The house
was tiny and clean, and in the correct catchment area for our school
of choice. Surprisingly the owner himself happened to be present at the
time of viewing so we were able to meet him in person and even have a
brief conversation before the next family to see the house, had arrived.*

*Nothing transpired until a week later, after all this prayer and
fasting had occurred. The solicitor's office called and told us that the
homeowner wanted to speak with us, directly. I called him back and he
asked why we hadn't rented his home. I told him of our predicament.
He said, "I really don't know why, but I feel compelled to help you."
He wanted to rent us his home, regardless of the rulings from the*

solicitor's office! Not only that, but he knocked fifty pounds off the monthly rent, too!

What you need to know, is that not only was this offer completely remarkable, but because houses were being rented the very day that they'd been advertised, it was truly miraculous that God had held the house for us, for more than a week!

At long last we had a home in Scotland. We were ecstatic until we realized that we had one teensy weensy little problem. Our container of belongings, which had been delayed, was originally a blessing but now a hindrance.

We didn't have anything with which to live ...
no plates or cutlery, no mats, blankets or pillows ... nothing!

Well, wouldn't you know it, after having attended just two different churches, once each, folks started showing up at our very empty house with things for us to use until our personal effects arrived! Praise God! We felt so blessed. Finally, with a rental agreement in hand, we could also acquire a bank account, or so we thought. Unfortunately, this didn't actually take place for yet another six weeks. Thank the Lord that some of our friends from Canada began to wire us money for groceries, or things would have been far worse.

God was definitely with us but there were days when I struggled with my desire to go back home. It's challenging to put into words; it felt as though I needed to run away, far away, as quickly as my short little legs would allow or else my heart would explode from the pain and discomfort. It literally took everything that I had and then some, to remain calm and not act on this anxiety. It was after one such occasion that God presented me with some pretty major correction, when He lovingly but firmly led me to Luke 9:62 which says,

"But Jesus said to him, 'No one, having put his hand to the plough, and looking back, is fit for the kingdom of God.'"

Ouch! That was sobering and stayed with me. Strangely enough, just a few lines after that scripture, is one that we encountered on a number of occasions after arriving in the U.K. It's the one that speaks of the need for labourers. Given that there had been a desperate plea for labourers in Scotland, it caused us to be quite puzzled by the resistance and suspicious nature that greeted us.

Now it needs to be said that the people of Scotland are lovely and friendly, so their suspicion wasn't anything overt, but rather something unspoken. It occurred to me that God had, indeed, responded to their prayers, sending quite a number of labourers and they (we) had responded, coming from Canada, the U.S., Australia, Switzerland, Holland, Ireland, England, Wales, South Africa and Poland to name just a few!

> I think that when these beautiful humble Scottish
> peoples prayed, what they wanted were labourers
> from Scotland and instead they got us.
> We weren't quite what they had in mind.

It just goes to show the truth in that old adage, "Be careful what you pray for!" Although we were feeling somewhat displaced and a little off balance in our new environment, we were also being given an unbelievable number of opportunities to share our faith. So, in pushing through and past the pain and anxiety, I kept my eyes fixed on the Lord and on the task before me.

After hearing our "accents," the number one question was always the same, "Where are you from?" followed by a puzzled, "Why would you move here?" Many of those we met couldn't understand why we had left Canada. The non-believers, in particular, described their lives and circumstances as being quite abysmal and regularly spoke to us of their desire to leave the area.

At first this seemed strange when considering the beauty of the landscape – the ocean, the mountains and the rich and honoured heritage. It also didn't jibe with the statistics that clearly stated Inverness was the fastest growing community in all of Europe. So in the natural, this seemed very odd, but in the spiritual it really wasn't strange at all, especially knowing and sensing firsthand the spiritual "heaviness" that was there.

It didn't take long to discover how this dark atmosphere had come to be. As we gained a deeper understanding of Inverness and its history, the battle of Culloden and the disturbing amount of high-level witchcraft present, it was clearly evident that this "darkness" had built up over many years. Curses had come upon this place as a result of generational sin, bloodshed and rampant demonic, druid and cult activity. It was alarming to note that much of this was accepted as normal and was considered to be "part of the culture," likely because it had been this way for so long.

Although responding to ongoing questions about our move from every person we met was a little uncomfortable, we also recognized it had been meticulously and wonderfully designed to be precisely as it was. It would have been far simpler to share reports of a fantastic new job or of a family member who had inspired this move, but that was not God's plan.

When asked by everyone from cab drivers and shop keepers to the school's staff and potential employers as to why we had moved, all we could say was … "God led us here." Even if we had attempted to give our answers a more palpable twist, we would have had no way of backing them up. So, for the time being, nice light conversations had become a thing of the past!

> These experiences, along with many others prior to this time,
> reaffirmed that being honest and humble in expressing our
> faith is vital.

I understand how awkward it can be to move from a place of private and personal faith to one of boldness, so I'm not talking about being pushy and overbearing, but instead being both forthcoming and sensitive, in love. Let's not be afraid to let others know that we are people of faith. Often the simplicity of saying this very thing will instigate a conversation, if not at the time, perhaps later on down the road. Once you have expressed your "position" so to speak, just be led by the Spirit as to what, if anything should follow.

> We're not selling Jesus. We're sharing. If we
> scare folks off then we've become a detriment
> to the faith, and that's not a good thing.

There's no particular "formula" for effectively sharing your faith and you probably have your own evangelism style, but because I've seen it done well and seen it executed poorly, I'd like to offer up a couple of suggestions. Essentially, the best way to speak into someone's life is to have a relationship with them. When we know people and they know us, there is a much better chance that they will be open to us and to the gospel. When a non-believer approaches me with a personal problem, if appropriate, I'll say "the only way that I'd know how to help with that, would be to share from a place of faith and I don't know how you'd feel about that."

Honestly, more often than not, this is acceptable to them because they likely trust me enough to share their hearts with me or they wouldn't have coveted my help in the first place. Remember, though, that in most cases we don't know the experiences these folks have had with faith or religion prior to our discussion, so we should exercise discernment, being wise and yet not wavering in what we know to be true.

We must be transparent about our own questions and struggles, yet confident that in Christ, we have found freedom, love, peace or whatever it is, that has fuelled the conversation. There are, of course, occasions when we come across those who are argumentative, and itching for a fight. In these cases, I endeavour to not engage, disallowing myself from being drawn into a debate.

> Early in my faith, I would have felt the need to
> "defend" God, but as time has passed,
> I can see that God is pretty good at taking care of Himself!

In speaking with a stranger about the things of God, we need to listen intently both to what the person is saying and also to what the Holy Spirit may be revealing to us. Perhaps we will receive a word of knowledge or be able to provide them with some prophetic insight. Maybe we'll simply be given the opportunity to meet a need. There are a lot of creative ways to evangelize but the main ingredient is love. Generally speaking what people crave is love, to be noticed and to matter.

In Scotland I had a great discussion with a complete stranger, a taxi driver. After establishing the reason for our move, I just left the topic alone, but he didn't. He wanted clarification.

"Are you religious?" he queried

"No, my faith is about relationship and not religion," I answered. More curious than ever, he asked "So, how does that work?"

"Well," I began, "I know Jesus personally. He is my Lord. I love Him and serve Him and He loves me more than I could ever love Him." I went on to share what it looks like to live for Jesus. Throughout this entire explanation, I allowed for purposeful gaps should it be too much for him and he require an escape hatch! He didn't want out. He wanted more! He told me he wasn't a Christian and he'd only been to church a couple of times; once he found it dry and boring but the other time he felt as though "the Reverend" was speaking right to him.

"He probably was!" I replied, which seemed to surprise him. "Have you heard of the Trinity, the Father, Son and Holy Spirit?" I continued. Indeed, he had. I explained how the Holy Spirit would have prompted the pastor to speak on something or refer to something that would touch his spirit. He was fascinated.

As we approached my destination, he shared with me that he'd be attending a funeral later on in the day and that I was the third or fourth person he'd met over the past few days who "knew God." He was wondering what it all meant. I asked for his name, told him I'd keep him in my prayers and he thanked me. Now that is the perfect example of a person to whom God is speaking and also a great illustration of how God provides us with opportunities to share our faith.

It is God who draws people unto Himself, not us.

When someone has reached the point of being open, willing, a softened heart, broken, and anxious to hear the truth, then we have discovered a soul that God is calling into relationship. We are now God's vessel to share with them, as led.

For those who haven't yet come to this place, it is unlikely that we will be able to make even a small dent in the wall they have built around themselves. We could actually cause them to withdraw from God even further, if we are not sensitive. Again, this is my perspective, based on my experiences.

Being bold is good but it must also be accompanied by sensitivity. Another key to evangelism would be healthy "persistence." This does not mean chasing them down but consistently showing unconditional love. If God prompts us to pray for, help or mentor someone, then let's be persistent in befriending them. We need to be slow to quit or give up on those whom God has put in our path. My dad excelled at going out of his way to ensure that the "invisible" ones had been "seen" not only by him, but by the One who created them. He made everyone feel as though they were significant.

The best way to share the love of Christ is to love.

I've told many a non-believer who was going through a difficult time that I would be praying for them. I can't recall having ever received a negative response. I've also discovered it's even more effective to *ask* if they would like prayer. What I believe happens is that when someone says "yes" to prayer, a very key word has just been spoken and subsequently heard in the heavenly realm. They have opened up a piece of their hearts to God, to Jesus and to the Holy Spirit in having given permission for prayer. That's the power of words, something I'll speak more on soon. This also shifts them into the position of seeking, rather than being pursued.

We all know what it's like to be hunted down and cornered by an overzealous salesman or an evangelist from another faith (or even our own). It's awkward and irritating. Let's not present Jesus to people this way. If they have agreed to prayer, then use some discernment in determining whether to pray with them right on the spot, wait, or simply pray for them on your own. Whatever seems right at the time is likely right, but commit to praying for them and remember to ask God to protect them and the seeds planted in Jesus' name. One other point to keep in mind is the need to remain humble. While people have questions and we have found the answer in Jesus we shouldn't be prideful.

> While we needed Jesus in the past, we still need Him today.

This is one of the reasons that Christians are often viewed as hypocritical or even as offensive, by non-believers. They see our imperfections and are put off when we stand before them as though we think ourselves "better." None of us is worthy, not *one*! Unfortunately, though, many Christians do believe themselves to be better! Ouch! I remember a speaker from the U.S. saying, "Why is it that the longer we are Christians, the less we think we need Jesus?" Again, ouch!! We need Jesus as much as the lost do and if we think we don't, then we ourselves are lost. We have been saved by grace and not by any other reason. We don't deserve salvation any more than the next person. No good deed or well-lived life brings us into relationship with Jesus. Let's maintain a position of humility, confessing our ongoing need for Jesus. I've found that people respond best to hearing the good news when we are truthful, honouring and authentic. Transparency is key and choosing our words wisely is imperative.

Power of Words

Words have astonishing power! It is with words that God called the world into being! We stand on God's Word and believe God keeps His Word, as it is written. This is our bread. This is what sustains us and brings us life. We are justified by our words, and by our words we are condemned. Words can be used to speak life or death. They can be used to build up or to rebuke. Thoughtless words can cause us to put away our dreams, while words that edify will encourage us beyond what we'd ever thought possible. That's big! Many folks don't recognize the significance of words and how vital it is that we watch the words with which we have stood in agreement.

When we agree with something someone has said and those words are not godly or edifying, we may have inadvertently cursed another person. Unfortunately, gossip is one of those sins that people don't take too seriously, making it one of Satan's more effective and frequently utilized weapons. Once again, Scripture says that death and life are in the power of the tongue. We have all found ourselves in awkward situations in which potentially hurtful conversation abounds, causing us to repent after the fact, remorseful at having participated. So while this is a somewhat universal issue, it doesn't make it any more right or any less damaging. We are still in error. Scripture says we will give an account for every idle word that we speak. Did you catch that? For every idle word, we will give an account. That is quite something, isn't it?! This is why I'm addressing the subject, because the harm that can be done to us and to others is far more devastating than what may be realized.

Unfortunately, I have been witness to Christians
who celebrated the losses, hurts or demise
of their brothers or sisters in Christ.

After one of our bigger concerts, word spread quickly that it had been a financial disappointment. What occurred next was something one might expect from a schoolyard bully. However, I'm not referring to an insensitive child, but rather a respected Christian woman who quite literally jumped for joy squealing with delight at our loss. It was particularly strange behaviour, given that she was fairly affluent and we were struggling to make ends meet.

At first I felt upset and distrustful but then God prompted me to pray for her. In the beginning, the prayers were simply carried out in obedience but as time passed, it became evident, even to me, that my heart toward her had softened.

About two years after the initial offense, she surprised me by offering our family some items that we needed for our home. Then, over time, prayers of support were added and eventually she even worked as a volunteer at one of our events. If you had told me that this sort of transformation and reconciliation would have taken place, I would have been dubious at best, but there it was!

It re-established in my heart the tremendous power of prayer.

It also caused me to contemplate the reason for such joy when loss or a fall occurs within the body of Christ. What I think happens is that one believer in a group is called to step up and out, this makes his or her friends very uncomfortable. Those watching may begin to see God's hand of favour, blessing and protection on this person and they immediately think to themselves "Why is that? This person isn't better than me. This person isn't perfect. Why is God using them?"

At this point, I am reminded of the story of Joseph and his brothers. His brothers would rather see Joseph dead or sold, than to see him blessed! Can you imagine? What seems to happen is that the onlookers believe they've somehow been abandoned by their brother, friend or acquaintance and so begin to speak out words of hatred. In so doing, they have cursed them.

Now, if bad things happen to their friend, they are actually happy. If their friend encounters trouble, they criticize all the more, saying "I told you that would happen." Well yes, they actually spoke it into being. They feel justified in their bad behaviour, confident that this trial will slow down or stop their friend's progress, which it probably did. How tremendously sad is this?! What I find so bewildering is that often these people aren't even interested in taking a step like the one their friend has, so then why be so hateful?

> Those who tear others down, who stand on the sidelines,
> spitefully attempting to destroy the dreams of others
> have no real interest in doing something positive themselves.

They have lost their way and they've also crippled the work of the godly. What a mess! Do you see what I mean about Satan's stronghold within the church family! Those who choose to remain "on the sidelines" need to guard against the urge to judge, criticize or hold others back. Not only is the one who is living by faith carrying a greater burden, but they are also on the enemy's radar, making their plight for Him all the more difficult.

I would encourage you to avoid becoming a tool in Satan's hand. I've watched in dismay the lack of grace shown to those who have stepped out of their comfort zone with a desire to be obedient, and then stumbled or fallen. Have the saints forgotten that they too have received grace? Why so quick to condemn those who have succumbed to the pressures of the world whilst desiring to serve. I'm not saying that those who have sinned, fallen or simply stumbled hold no accountability or responsibility, but what I am saying is that the "gossipers" are making things more difficult.

It is often the Christian friends or "on-lookers"
who allow the enemy to use them in despicable ways.

They have fallen into a trap set by the enemy. While they ridicule and judge the one who has been hurt or fallen, they haven't recognized the fact that they have not only aided in it through word curses or by other means, but that they themselves have also fallen. Worse yet, their fall can't even be attributed to godly activity, but in fact, quite the opposite! They have actually sided with the enemy by acting or speaking on his behalf. No one wins, except the devil.

Don't allow yourself to fall into this trap. The next time you feel compelled to say, "I told you that would happen," think about what that statement means. It could mean that you actually helped to make it happen - making you a part of the problem, not a part of the solution. Remember too, that you will be judged by the same measure that you have judged. It has a boomerang effect so be vigilant and self-aware.

If you really feel that you must express yourself about something then *please*, prior to doing so, diligently seek the Lord in prayer and in the Word. Ensure that your heart, thoughts and motives are clean and pure. Sometimes the judgment or "sense" in our hearts about another person is actually about us! It could be Holy Spirit conviction that's been placed within us, intended for our own refinement and not, in fact, meant for another. Search yourself before speaking out potentially hurtful words. There have been occasions when I have been given a word of "caution" or "rebuke" that didn't line up with what God was showing me. I prayed for clarity and in more than one case, it turned out that the word given was either intended for the person who gave it to me or was a word of warning to me, in reference to the one who had spoken it to me!

Those who prophesy only "prophesy" and "know" in part.

They may indeed have a "word" for you but they may also be prone to tossing in a couple of their own thoughts, fleshly thoughts, not spiritual thoughts. The most powerful prophetic words that I have received in my lifetime have been from strangers. These words were accurate and "struck a chord" demonstrating to me that they were from the Lord. As a general rule, it is always best to exercise caution before speaking, making certain that our words impart grace to the hearers.

Another thought for your consideration is to watch when, where, how and why we use scripture in our prayer lives. I know that sounds strange, so allow me to share some revelation in relation to this concept. I'm going to use Isaiah 54:17a as my example: *"No weapon formed against you shall prosper, and every tongue which rises against you in judgment you shall condemn. This is the heritage of the servants of the Lord ..."*

I've heard many people incorporate this Scripture into their prayer lives, changing and inserting words to make it more personal. (For example: no weapon formed against *me* shall prosper ...). What's interesting to note is that many do not notice that the Scripture speaks of *"every* tongue" that rises against us. Do you realize that when you are praying this, you could be heaping coals of judgment and condemnation upon yourself, given that you are praying against "every" word that has been spoken against you? "Every word spoken against you" would include the words you have spoken against yourself. This prayer could also be causing judgment to come upon your spouse, children, siblings, parents or friends for the words they have spoken against you in a moment of anger or misunderstanding.

I'm not speaking against the Scripture, merely pointing out that in this instance it might be better to request that those who are rising against you receive forgiveness, rather than condemnation.

When we pray this scripture, we are usually thinking about what our "enemies" are saying against us, not what we are saying against ourselves or against others. Even so, let's not forget that scripture also instructs us to bless those who curse. I only communicate this, so that our prayers become more thoughtful and careful.

Oftentimes, the words we speak into being are completely contrary to what we actually desire to see occur. When I am frustrated or angry and say something like "Everything I do seems to go wrong," I have spoken a curse against myself. What happens next is that everything I do starts to go wrong. I blame God when in fact it's simply a self-fulfilling prophecy being realized! Again, we should make every effort to speak words of life and not words of death.

Use words that bless, not words that curse.

When walking by faith I realize there are times when it seems as though too much is coming at us from too many sources and it's difficult to determine what is of God and what isn't. When receiving input or "advice," I've learned that it's not necessary to "judge" those giving the counsel but rather to examine their fruit. "You will know them by their fruits ... every good tree bears good fruit, but a bad tree bears bad fruit" (Matthew 7:16a, 17).

Just as you'd likely not accept counsel on parenting from someone whose children are unruly and disrespectful, you should also carefully consider and watch from whom you receive any spiritual input by first examining their fruit. All good fruit that you see in a person of faith is because it came from the Lord.

"... love your enemies, bless those who curse you,
do good to those who hate you, and pray for those
who spitefully use you and persecute you ..."
—Matthew 5:44

Chapter 7

REALITY OF FAITH

God's Plan

I THANK GOD that amidst the trials of life, I have chosen to make every effort to smile and maintain a sense of humour. The morning that our overseas container arrived at our very empty home in Scotland brought huge relief, but was also a comedy of errors!

As I consumed the last of my cereal, I felt certain that I'd heard the sounds of a large vehicle idling out in front of our house. Surely it wasn't our moving truck … this was too early – one hour too early! I ran to the window and realized that it was, indeed, our truck and with it, came exceedingly tight deadlines. I was yelling for Kevin all the while hoping that our sleeping teenagers would hear my frantic cries for help and get up and out of bed. I went outside to speak with the driver who told me that, as anticipated, we were only being given three hours to empty an extraordinarily full container. After that, we'd be charged an additional fee. The clock was ticking and my heart was racing …

Determined that we use our time wisely, I asked the driver to lower the back of the truck, so that it would be all prepared for unloading. The driver gave me one of those heart-stopping, blank, mystified gazes.

I repeated my request explaining to him, "You see when we packed the container in Canada, it was on the ground."

At this point I realized that the problem had nothing to do with my accent nor did it have anything to do with his understanding my English but with the harsh reality that there was no way to lower the truck and … there was no ramp! This meant that we needed to unload it the way it was numerous feet off the ground. After recovering from the shock of what I'd just heard, we noticed that the seal which was on the lock for the overseas trip needed to be removed and of course, we had no tools (and neither did the driver!). I frantically ran inside, grabbed my recently acquired mobile, to call one of our new friends for help while Kevin studied the lock, attempting to come up with a plan as to how to remove it. Fifteen minutes passed before our very sweet seventy-five-year-old friend arrived, decked out in coveralls and a boot full (trunk full) of tools. Bless him!

As he and Kevin madly worked to remove the seal, the kids got dressed and I paced and prayed. This whole process took about forty minutes of our precious time. Now, with less than two and a half hours remaining, we had to lift everything out of the truck which was about four feet above the ground with only two, Kevin and our son, being fully capable of this feat for more than half of what was in the truck. Well, suffice it to say this was challenging, humorous and traumatic all at the same time but we got the job done, and with ten minutes to spare.

Now imagine this, the truck is driving away and our yard, carport and sidewalk are completely littered with furniture, musical instruments, nearly two hundred boxes and more, all strewn in and around the smallest abode that Kevin and I have ever called 'home' since getting married and, well you get the picture! We could almost hear the neighbours bemoaning the fact that some crazy foreigners with a lot of "rubbish" had just moved into the area.

Given that there are no basements, only attics
or lofts, small doors and entranceways, we
couldn't even get our sofa into the house!

And so, after numerous attempts by every available means - even through windows, we gave up and gave the sofa away. Hopefully someone in the Highlands is now enjoying our well-travelled sofa. During all the madness, we finally got our telephone and internet connected, which allowed us to contact family and friends. This was a huge relief, especially given the news that I'd received from home, via email, about my Dad's cancer diagnosis. I was terribly frustrated by my "helplessness" in that situation and was beginning to experience more angst than joy. I found myself becoming emotionally drained and although we had seen some break-through, we were burdened with grief over my Dad's illness and my Mom's struggle in caring for him single-handedly.

We still didn't have jobs and everything from that perspective was moving at an insufferably slow rate of speed. It was incomprehensible to us as to why God would choose to move us to a place where there seemed to be absolutely no work for us and not even any foreseeable opportunities that lined up with our skill-sets. We hadn't met any professional musicians and were told in no uncertain terms, that "what had worked in Canada, wouldn't work in Inverness." We met with funding organizations, new business help groups and key folks in the arts. Nothing positive transpired. We were continually being told what we could *not* do. We were anxious for even a glimmer of hope, but none came!

There also seemed to be an onslaught of adversity, as nearly every correspondence from Canada was in relation to something tragic; deaths, relational difficulties, and on and on it went. The pull toward home was strong and all we could do was cast our burdens on Jesus and pray, a lot. We also began to receive a very strong sense that there was still more required of us. We not only needed to lay down our lives, country, family, friends, what little financial stability we had (along with everything we'd known), but …

He also wanted us to lay down our dreams,
our gifts and abilities, too.

I tell you that, in all honesty, this was about all we could take! I was gripped by an overwhelming sadness that resulted in a personal "death." We pacified ourselves with the fact that we hadn't come this far to not go the distance. We also recognized that this wasn't simply refining, it was also testing. Were we prepared to literally lay it all down, regardless of the cost? "Yes" we were, but even so, it was a devastating time and a painful process. "Until the time that his Word came to pass, the Word of the Lord tested him" (Psalm 105:19).

What ensued was a period of mourning as we laid down not just our gifts and abilities but the passion we had to serve God with those gifts, knowing that He wanted to do a "new thing," We didn't know what that new thing was, only that it was necessary that we die to, and let go of, how we had been used in the past, so that He could accomplish His goals in His way and not in ours. It was imperative that we release the past knowing God can make a road in the desert, creating something wonderful out of nothing at all. We had to trust that God was going to finish what He had started. Despite our best efforts we still, on occasion, found ourselves questioning if we had heard correctly.

Was Inverness actually the place God had chosen for us?

Then, as if right on cue, we heard from Kevin's mom. She was quivering with excitement. Apparently, she had come across a very old locket that she had received as a child. Upon closer scrutiny, she noticed a small bit of paper peeking out from beneath the cotton under the locket, something that in seventy years she had never before seen! She carefully unfolded the delicate and yellowed paper, which turned out to be a clipping from an old newspaper. It was an obituary that revealed some stunning information. What this seemingly insignificant little piece of paper revealed was something so crucial that we never again questioned our location!

What she read knocked her (and our) socks off. She discovered that her great, great grandfather had lived and died in ... wait for it ... Inverness! Now, how wild is that? Most of the focus up until this time had been on my ancestry, on my grandparents, both of whom were from Huntly, which is about sixty miles from Inverness. What this meant was that unbeknownst to us, God had sent us directly to the very city of Kevin's heritage with absolutely *no* prior knowledge of this critical piece of information! This was completely God, working in hidden ways that we never could have conjured up on our own! As one friend so aptly put it,

"God writes the best stories."

How true! And they are the best because He's breathed life into them and His fingerprints are all over them! This extraordinarily precious gift had been left unwrapped, not to be revealed until this moment in time as an encouragement to us that we were indeed, in the correct location and that we had, indeed, heard from the Lord!

It's tremendous that we received this piece of good news, because the word from my parents continued to be discouraging. We were praying for my Dad's healing and strength for my Mom and we were running out of money with each passing day. We were barely hanging on and then, yet another attack, almost like a repeat of what we'd seen before – angry notes from a friend about our decision to move, our call to live by faith. This was something they felt had put our family in serious jeopardy. The timing could not have been worse. Of course, I knew in an instant that this blast of judgment was simply a fleshly response from one who didn't understand but regardless, it was still hurtful. It caused me to reflect on all the questioning and persecution that we'd received since venturing out in faith.

Friends wondered why we'd been called to a depth of faith that required we endure these hardships, and they hadn't. That's a difficult one, because only God can respond to a question like that. There could be any number of reasons, the most obvious being that *all* Christians are actually called to a deep commitment of faith, but many have opted out. One thing I do know is that I have had a blessed life with a rich and wonderful childhood. I didn't have to spend the second third of my life recovering from the first part of my life. That isn't to say that I haven't had my share of struggles but it's apparent that I have been given much, and therefore much has been required of me.

> "For everyone to whom much is given,
> from him much will be required ..."
> —Luke 12:48

In terms of the hardships I still quite simply believe that trouble comes as part and parcel of the faith walk. We are required to live in obedience and although there may be difficult days, it's all about knowing and trusting that God has it in hand. That said, there have been many occasions when my husband and I have put ourselves "out there", believing in faith, waiting for our God, our source to show up and He's been late! OK, let me clarify that; He's been late from my perspective. Obviously, we're still alive and well. We're still here, so He must have done something along the way to rescue us, but frequently it was not according to our liking or our timelines. It was, however, according to *His* plan.

Despite my best efforts to squelch any and all negative feelings, the truth was that I could feel anxiety rising up in me. The rent was due and we absolutely didn't have it. We were trusting in faith but time was up! This would be the second month in a row we had been unable to pay! I shuddered to think what the landlord would say when I broke the news to him. I felt like such a terrible witness and reprimanded myself, heaping shame and guilt on top of the existing humiliation.

This man had been so good to us. Just the fact that he'd allowed us to move in, without jobs, no U.K. history and no bank account was extraordinary but now we were asking for something over the top. We were asking for grace! Thank the Lord that my fears of being homeless and on the street lifted when this remarkable man, yet again, extended favour and also understanding.

Days and weeks passed; in fact, almost another full month went by before, at long last, God provided! I couldn't contact the landlord fast enough. I told him that a friend had given us a gift so that we could pay all the rent money owed. He was genuinely touched and told us what incredible friends we had. This we knew, but then he said something completely unexpected. He told us he admired us and the lives we were living. What? How could this be? I had convinced myself that our testimony was abysmal but God was proving me wrong.

I have often thought about what it must have been like for Mary and Martha when their brother Lazarus took ill. They sent for Jesus, and by all accounts Jesus was late, very late, because by the time He arrived, Lazarus had been dead four days. And yet, as the Bible shows us Jesus got there in time! Given the length of time that Lazarus had been in the tomb, there was no doubt as to his "status." When Jesus brought him back to life, the Father was glorified even more than if Jesus had simply healed him. This was clearly more magnificent! This was how God chose to realize His plan in this particular instance.

Still, I think that Mary and Martha must have felt it would have saved them a lot of grief if Jesus had just shown up when they wanted Him to show up. At times like these we must remember our God is a Sovereign God and not one to be manipulated. He knows and decides what is best.

For a couple who isn't very materialistic or money-oriented, we've cried out to God more than our fair share about this very concern. I have often moaned about the level of sacrifice that's been required and have absolutely detested how it has attempted to steal my time, my joy and my focus. I have even found myself concerned with how, by living on the edge, we would ever be able to leave our children an inheritance. I frequently remember telling God I had reached the end of myself, begging for help and still, nothing would change. Finally, one day I could take it no longer. I wept and prayed,

> "I'm at the end of my rope, Lord, and I don't want you to give me more rope like you always do. I need revelation, so that I can get past this. It's been ten years of scraping by and I can't take it for another day."

Finally, after so much pain and so much suffering, I received insight. Until I trusted Him without reserve, He would not trust me with any further assignments or people or anything!

I had to trust in faith, day in and day out, week in and week out, for Him to provide for our every need; our food, our rent and for our bills to be paid!

Because I had to believe for these everyday needs, in faith, I couldn't be double-minded at *any* time or in *any* way about *any* thing. I needed to believe with all assurance that He would care for us, even though in the natural it looked to be impossible. I had to give up worrying, being self-sufficient and completely humble myself before God. Whoa! Here we were in a new country amidst virtual strangers or people we'd only known for a very short time, and I needed to trust that we'd be cared for.

Well, He's good to His Word and although in the natural we were long past the point of being on "the edge," He really did take care of us and I can honestly testify that it was the first time since beginning this walk of faith that I'd had little to no worries or anxieties in terms of provision. Through this entire season, I must reiterate the fact that we had no backing, no credit cards and no financial support of any kind but … we did have God!

Once we had jumped off the edge of the cliff and found ourselves in that crazy free fall, although frightening to the naked eye, it was freeing to the soul.

So even when our needs mounted and in the flesh it appeared as though the problems before us were too great to bear, I focused on Christ and on His sacrifice. I thought of Moses and all those who were with him in the desert. God fed about three million people every day for forty years. I understand that was calculated to be approximately fifteen hundred tons of food and eleven million gallons of water, each and every day. Their clothes never wore out and their sandals always fit! I figured if God was able to do that, then He'd be able to feed, clothe and provide shelter for our little family which He did and does! "And my God shall supply all your need according to His riches in glory by Christ Jesus" (Philippians 4:19).

Clink. Clank. Clunk. Coins were being emptied into an old, chipped and somewhat unremarkable mug, which had found its place on the counter in our bright, cheery little blue and white kitchen. The mug was meant to contain bus fare for our kids so that they could travel to and from school on the city bus.

A friend had stopped by and noticed that it was once again empty. Although our friend had very few resources himself, he had "donated" to the cause! This was something that seemed to have become a regular occurrence. Money anonymously popped through our mail slot, new friends stopping in to drive us to the store to collect some groceries or even coming by to mow the lawn. There were even occasions when a local church (not our own) arranged to have groceries delivered to us! Surprise lunches and warm invitations to go sightseeing were aplenty! The generosity overwhelmed and humbled us.

We had come with hearts to help and serve and instead found ourselves being helped. What I later realized, was that we were actually sowing into one another's lives. We needed each other and while the situation was contrary to our nature, it was pleasing to the Lord.

The Body

"In the world you will have tribulation; but be of good cheer, I have overcome the world" (John 16:33b). Living in this world can be difficult, but how could it be any other way? After all, the world operates one way and those of us, who are in Christ, live, think and believe something diametrically opposed. So as we do our best to navigate our way through life, living God's way in an environment that is completely contrary to His, it's not surprising that we can and will experience pain and difficulties. The victory comes in knowing …

"... He who is in you is greater than he who is in the world."
—1 John 4:4

Throughout those initial weeks in Scotland, we attended a number of different churches, but none seemed like a good fit. Then one day, at a medical appointment, I was pleasantly surprised to learn that my doctor was a Christian! She invited us to her church and so the following Sunday we mapped out our bus route and off we went.

We were no sooner seated in the church's meeting hall, when we were greeted by one of the leaders, who quickly recognized we had not located the church we were seeking. Well, as only God can direct these things, although it wasn't the church *we'd* planned to attend, it was in fact, the one God had destined for us to belong! This church was full to overflowing with some of the most passionate, kind-hearted and generous people we'd ever met and subsequently, ever known. We had found our new church home.

Among these believers we were astonished to find others, like ourselves, who had been sent from the nations. Did you catch that? There were others who had been sent to Inverness – just like us! We weren't an anomaly after all! What an incredible blessing it was to come across people, passionate for God, who had moved without jobs or homes or friends, but when asked to "go," went, just like us! It not only helped us to feel much less alone in our call and in our walk, but it was exciting to consider the possibilities of what God was doing. Natives of Scotland, those who'd arrived from other nations as led, and those of us from other nations who, in essence had "re-emigrated," had been assembled.

> I felt as though our commander in chief had gathered His troops, was moving us into place and we, His trusting warriors, were anxiously awaiting further instruction.

I'm also fascinated by the fact that we are a musical family, knowing full well how throughout scripture, the musicians, the worshiping warriors, went before the army. I felt so blessed and humbled to be among those called to this impending move of God.

After a number of revelatory conversations with the Scots, we learned that in 1967 American missionary, Jean Darnall, while living in England, had a vision of a time of spiritual awakening in the British Isles. She saw revival fires that God lighted from the top of Scotland, through the highlands and downward over England, to land's end. Here we were, decades later, able to see that many of the key components of this vision were coming to fruition, bringing us even closer to this new thing that God was planning to execute. We were tremendously excited!

In our flesh we had hoped to have a clearer, more comprehensive picture of "the plan" and "our role." Then one day while praying with our Scottish friends, we received understanding as to why God had hidden His plan from us. Ultimately, it was for our own protection, because although we had no idea as to what was to transpire, neither did the enemy! What a fantastic strategy! What this meant, though, was that in order for God's plan to be effective, it was up to us to live obediently and prayerfully exclusively by faith, trusting without seeing, day in and day out.

> He had moved us into a new level of
> faith, protection and provision!

How comforting it was to see that God had clearly gone before us, preparing the people, the place, the spiritual atmosphere and more. One of our new and very dear friends, a true "Invernesian," had also received a personally life-changing word from the Lord fourteen years prior to our appearance. She had been informed that God was planning to send people from the nations and that her role was to pray, watch for and welcome us. So for all these years, she had been praying into the situation, long before having ever laid eyes on us, in faith and in anticipation of our arrival.

Throughout our time in Scotland she and her family consistently, diligently, warmly and generously cared for those of us who had been sent. She had been shown that we "foreigners" were able to provide something that those who had lived in Scotland throughout their lives could not, acknowledging that "a prophet has no honour in his own country."

This is why God was and is, sending people to other nations. Often in our own home or country, our gifts can be minimized or rationalized away, ultimately resulting in God not being glorified and in our not being used to the fullest. If Jesus Himself was reduced to being seen as "just the carpenter's son" in His homeland, then how much more we?! God wants to use us fully and completely and sometimes this is not possible in our communities or countries of origin. This being the case, He sends us to others or others to us. He speaks of this in the book of Isaiah when he proclaims that it is the sons of foreigners who will build up their walls.

As God decidedly and deliberately moves people around, sometimes to new and faraway lands, it will stir things up! People may misunderstand what He is doing and what His children are called to, but rest assured, the Lord has a plan. We must all be watchful and mindful that we not miss out on what our role in that plan might be; whether it is to go, to encourage, to pray, to welcome or to help. Together, as led by Christ, we can be a part of His kingdom work.

"Then Jesus said to them ... as the Father
has sent me, I also send you."
—John 20:2

While in Scotland we were encouraged to see people from virtually every denomination gathering together to pray in groups and in ways like we'd never seen before. God was at work. Many Christians went on regular prayer walks, praying through the city, over the hills and wherever sent. There was a group of volunteer street pastors who worked in partnership with the local constabulary (police) to provide folks with a listening ear and to help with keeping the peace. A vibrant "healing on the streets" ministry took place every week in the town centre with members from a number of churches who worked together with a shared cause on their hearts. It was inspiring to see the unity.

Something positively wonderful happens when unity exists.

When walls come down and Christians come together in agreement, we can see God's power at work, making it possible for us to do and experience even greater things. In the book of Ecclesiastes, we hear how difficult it is to break a threefold cord. There is strength and power in standing and working together. When we do this, I am convinced that God is smiling. After all, when one member suffers, all suffer and when one is honoured, all rejoice. It's teamwork. It's also entirely more fun when we are able to serve alongside positive, faith-filled, destiny-driven people who love the Lord.

I am so delighted we have a close-knit family. We enjoy one another's company whether it involves sharing a meal, playing a board game, vacationing, shopping, watching a movie together, time at the lake, working events or, my personal favourite, playing music. To share a passion for music and Christ in one activity as a family is such a blessing. Although we must weather the "von Andrews" jokes (the Sound of Music ... again?) and the fact that it's not particularly cool for youth to be playing music with their parents, I have to say, it has been a really great thing!

> Unity combined with a sense of humour has been vitally
> important to our family.

It's a massive responsibility to raise children in a world that has turned its back on God, prayer, respect of self and others, morals, ethics and the family unit. Teaching our kids to live faith-filled, Christ-like lives under these conditions can be, and is, arduous.

To remain focused on what we know to be true, pure, right and lovely *and* still function in this world is the goal. Our kids have flaws and struggles, just as we all do, but over the years they have been such a blessing and joy, mostly because of God's grace and partly because we have invested a great deal into them, their spiritual lives and their sense of security. We may have struggled financially, but our children have always had access to Mom and Dad. They've been given healthy boundaries, direction, consistency, love, prayer, guidance, encouragement and more. This is not to commend ourselves, but to say that raising godly kids in this world requires diligence, time and energy. We determined early on, that the best way to have input into their lives was to be with them … a lot!

In order for one of us to always be available, meant that creativity, careful scheduling, out-of-the-box thinking and sacrifice were required. Usually both parents must work in order to make ends meet. This is the way of the world's economy and so we did just that for many years but through it all, found inventive ways to manage our time, choosing our jobs carefully, purposefully and prayerfully, so that one of us was always around for the children.

It's not God's plan that today's young people receive the ragged remnants of our patience, time and energy. It's the devil who is attempting to rule this world and he is the one who has parents running here, there and everywhere, with activities, clubs, gadgets and electronics all of which, attempt to steal us away from our children or them away from us. Let's give them less stuff, fewer activities and a calmer, more peaceful us!

> It's a lie of the enemy that says stuff and busyness
> are of more value to your children than *you* are!

When parents are absent, distracted or exhausted, they need to stop and consider what values are being fed into their children's lives and by whom. There is a whole cause and effect phenomenon going on here. Although parents may get away with being inattentive for a while, over time these choices will become apparent in the behaviour of their children. I'm convinced that it's easier to gently and lovingly shape a child along the way than it is to whip a neglected and disgruntled teen into shape later. "Train up a child in the way he should go and when he is old he will not depart from it" (Proverbs 22:6). This is God's way but again, the world operates contrary to God.

If you find that you have been seduced into the world's way of thinking or maybe you are in a "no win" situation that has you spiralling downwards or out of control, it could be of great value for you to think beyond that which has already been tried and failed. Look for God's solutions. Ask God for creative ways to solve your dilemma.

When living in this world, the Bible says it's as though we are aliens here, but the good news is that, even if we don't "fit" here, when the time comes, we're gonna "fit" in heaven! In the meantime though, we do need to function here and to do so effectively, we must remind ourselves that it's not flesh and blood (people) with whom we struggle, but the principalities and powers of darkness (Satan). When living for Christ, we have overcome the darkness. That which desires to drag us down has no power over us. We must remind ourselves of this fact and endeavour to live according to the Spirit and not the flesh.

The responses of the flesh are not the same as those of the Spirit. As His children, we are required to love and forgive, to be patient and kind, not bitter, resentful or rebellious. So, while it's difficult not to be offended or hurt when attacked for our faith, especially by someone who knows the Lord, we must take the "high road," We're all just a bunch of regular folk doing our best to make it through this life. Sometimes we get it right and sometimes we don't, but as long as we keep growing and learning we can rest assured that we will know more today than we did yesterday and less today than we will tomorrow!

Throughout our journey of faith, we became acutely aware of the fact God had called us to walk out a measure of faith that we, ourselves, had never before witnessed first-hand. Seeking and searching for direction, answers and meaning without sight meant working through a wide range of thoughts and emotions with only the Scriptures, the Holy Spirit and less dramatic experiences from the past to guide us on our way. It meant re-evaluating how we viewed "faith" and then, on a daily basis, a continual dying to self. Although more was required of us than we had within us, we continued to trust that the Lord would lead us into His plans and purposes, which He did and still does.

The Cost

And so, after only two months in Scotland, I knew that I needed to go back to Canada to see my mom and dad and do whatever I could to help with my dad, who was failing in his health. I was gifted with a return ticket and so, gratefully and sorrowfully departed, hoping that I could be of some assistance to my mom. When I arrived at my parent's door after the twenty-three hour journey, I was met with the startling news that my dad had deteriorated more quickly than I'd anticipated and had been taken by ambulance to the hospital *while* I was en route to Canada. What ensued was just two precious days at my beloved dad's bedside.

These are days I would not trade for anything. Quietly and peacefully, after all the songs had been sung, the prayers had been prayed and the words had been spoken, he passed graciously and courageously from this life to the next, ever and always a man that I will love and admire until the day that I join him in glory. He taught me enough to fill the pages of another book, mostly by what he modelled and who he was; a man of great faith, to whom not one person he encountered was insignificant or forgotten. He was a very real example of a man after God's own heart, faithful, loving and courageous. I miss you, Dad! Your legacy lives on and we will endeavour to honour you and your memory by serving, without reserve, the God of Abraham, Isaac, Jacob and Ross!

After all the arrangements had been made, the memorial service was over and some of the details had been sorted around, it was time for me to go. It was heart-wrenching to leave my mom, knowing that once my brother and aunt had departed, she would be on her own. Saying good-bye to our daughter and her family yet again, was also difficult. Still, I needed to get back to Scotland. It had been painful for Kevin and the rest of the family left to mourn on their own, from such a great distance, this man who had impacted us all so significantly.

The international departures area was, as I imagine it usually is, a steady stream of busy travellers, some more tired than others but all with a focused determination to reach their desired destinations. I was in a fog. I sat down in a quiet area as tears uncontrollably poured down my face, memories of my dad flooding my mind and heart.

It hit me like a ton of bricks as I sat there, at the Vancouver airport, remembering the look on his face as we'd left for Scotland. He had been right. The sadness he'd experienced was, as it turned out, justified. It was, in fact, the last time he would see Kevin and three of his grandchildren. Had he known something that I'd been blind to see? My heart ached.

It was distressing to think that I would never again, on this earth, see him there, standing together with my mom, cheering us on; that I would not be able to see that encouraging smile or never again feel the warmth and comfort that came from his reassuring hugs. My protector and prayer warrior, our patriarch and godly example had gone on to a better place. I was grateful beyond words to have had such an extraordinary father but the intense pain, as a result of this loss, was real and at least for today, it was far too difficult to contain.

I wondered how my family would be and how I would feel upon my return to Scotland after all that had taken place. Strangely, I had a sense of "coming home" and this genuinely surprised me. By the time I'd gotten back to Inverness, it was very close to Christmas, which meant I was immediately inundated with all the usual preparations of the season.

Amidst the hustle and bustle, the processing of what had just taken place and the grieving, I had a rather healing revelation from God. He spoke into my heart the reason for the urgency in getting us to Scotland prior to my Dad's diagnosis. Had we known about the severity of my dad's illness while we were still in Canada, we likely would have moved to British Columbia and ignored the call to Scotland. He didn't want us to set Scotland aside. Scotland was where we needed to be and although deeply concerned for all those we'd left behind, we knew it was necessary that we release them and entrust them to God, knowing He would care for them, just as He was caring for us. Yes, the cost was dear but we also knew that

> while there is a significant and undeniable cost in serving Jesus, there is also a substantial cost to serving the devil.

151

I would far rather suffer while doing good than to suffer while doing or serving that which is evil or faithless. As we stand firm in our faith, especially in the midst of trials, we will grow. It's easy to have faith when things are going well for us, but will we remain steadfast when our faith is tested? Are we truly willing to "go to the ends of the earth" for Him? Will we actually *do* all those things we sing about in times of worship or are they just empty words that we say or sing but don't really mean?

> What happens when the rubber meets the road
> and God asks us to fit into His plans rather
> than us expecting Him to bless ours?

This is when we truly make a sacrifice of praise – when, perhaps, we don't "feel" like it. We've persevered through the struggles and the pain. We've reaped because we've sown, and that's a biblical principle, but again, there is cost associated with this walk. Jesus asks us to consider if we have enough commitment to be His disciples. We need to count the cost and think about what it is to bear this cross and whether or not we are willing to leave all else and follow.

> "For which of you, intending to build a tower,
> does not sit down first and count the cost, whether
> he has enough to finish it – lest after he has laid
> the foundation and is not able to finish it."
> —Luke 14:28

In Matthew 10:39, Jesus says, "He who finds his life will lose it, and he who loses his life for My sake will find it." The bright side is that although there is a cost, in the end, we are rewarded. When we sacrifice all, we will gain all. Once I leave this earth, I *know* where I will spend eternity and it will be with Jesus, so when counting the cost, regardless of what happens to me here on earth, I know where I'll end up and that makes the cost seem really reasonable!

So why walk by faith? It sounds a little scary. Well, yes it can be, but there's also a whole lot of beauty in serving. There is far more that is good and lovely in this walk than that which is negative. We really need to grasp the fact that in serving and bringing glory, honour and praise to the Father, Son and Holy Spirit, we are blessed. He is absolutely passionate about seeing us brought into His fullness, and His image. So the rough patches are strictly meant for our good. God would never hurt us or harm us. We are precious in His sight. We are His handiwork. We are loved and we matter! We bring Him pure joy. He delights in us.

A number of years back, one of our daughters, who was only about two or three years old at the time, was at the playground. It was a beautiful sunny afternoon and she was playing in the sand amidst all the other children. I was seated on a park bench watching her whilst attending to our youngest. Although in plain view, she began calling for me, "Mom, Mom, Mom" over and over again, giving me no opportunity whatsoever to respond. By the time I had a chance to say "yes", every other mom was now alerted to my little girl, standing in the middle of everything and everyone, her long blonde hair blowing in the gentle breeze. Again, she said "Mom, watch me!" At this point, *everyone* was watching! Then she did absolutely nothing. Well, actually, she posed and that was it! From that moment on, we called her our "watch me, child." It made me, and everyone else, chuckle. But, you know, I think God would have loved that! He just enjoys watching us.

> We don't have to be doing anything special or spectacular for
> Him to take pleasure in us.

No matter our age, we make Him smile, simply because we are His children and He is our Heavenly Father. What a beautiful and comforting thought! In fact, He is all that we will ever need. He is our salvation (Romans 3:22-25, Romans 1:16); refuge, strength (Psalm 46:1); shield (Proverbs 30:5); fortress (Psalm 31:2); rock (2 Samuel 22:32-24); provider, source (Matthew 6:25); creator, maker, helper (Isaiah 40:28, 29, Psalm 121:1, 2); Lord of Lords, King of Kings (Revelation 19:16b); comforter (2 Corinthians 1:4); and that's just the beginning!

There is so much more to this awesome relationship and although we have a tendency to focus on the "here and now," knowing Him is also about the redemption we have received through faith in Him (Ephesians 1:7). It's about living every moment unto eternity with Him (Romans 6:23). It's about being lost without Him (Romans 10:9, 10). It's about His gift of salvation (Ephesians 2:8). It's all about Him and what He's done for us and not the other way around! Doesn't that make you want to serve Him with everything you've got? And in the end, everything you've got is everything He's given you!

A Good Testimony

We are told in scripture to obtain a good testimony so that we can share our stories and encourage others. Hearing how God has worked in the lives of those around us has the ability to boost our faith. It blesses us and motivates us to walk out our own destinies with passion and conviction.

It increases our expectancy about what God can and will do. I love to hear dramatic conversion stories, but I more thoroughly enjoy hearing "faith" stories. I am drawn to hearing about the work God is doing in the lives of the faithful, how they have been made over-comers in the face of adversity, and the ways in which the Lord's goodness and mercy has been revealed through them. I've noticed that many Christians are hesitant to share their stories, believing they have nothing "exciting" to say or that their testimonies are "boring." No! These testimonies are not boring. Just because you've never been a drug addict, a terrorist or a victim of slavery doesn't mean that God isn't doing a miraculous work in and through you. If you've come from a solid Christian background, then you have a testimony of perseverance in the faith and you are enjoying the benefits of the spiritual cleaning and faithfulness of those who've gone before you. Your "boring" life will hearten those who are trying to make a better life for their children. The testimony of your ancestors is part of your testimony. If you have been protected from evil because of your heritage, that is truly good news!

My conversion story at the age of twelve is a tame tale and yet I think that my adventure in faith has been something worth sharing. If the only good testimony we have is our salvation story, then we have remained a baby in the faith. Let's move beyond the infant stage and into a maturity of faith that declares the immenseness and extravagance of God working in us and through us on a daily basis. The added bonus in all of this is that the more we speak about our faith, the more real it becomes to us.

In speaking it out, we build up our own faith and we are encouraged. Yes, even as we listen to our own voices proclaiming His truths we are lifted and edified, reminded over and over again of the mighty God we serve and then, remarkably, we grow in faith! We also give way to that "great cloud of witnesses" who are able to add their "amen."

> God has a plan and a purpose for each one of us.
> We need to determine what that plan is and then do it!

My husband and I are just regular folks who were called to a people, a place and a purpose as directed by our Lord and Saviour and because we obeyed, we have a testimony. As we seek after Him and follow Him, He provides us with information, strategy and assignments on what I call a "need to know" basis. When we arrived in Scotland, we were acutely aware of the fact that we had been removed from all that was familiar. Although difficult, we were also unencumbered by the usual distractions of life. This meant we were more easily able to hear and act in obedience to what was being communicated from on high. We didn't need to battle the pressures that can come from both personal and cultural expectations. As Canadians in Scotland, we were given extraordinary latitude and grace if we failed to do things the "Scottish way." This, however, didn't necessarily mean that we were doing things the "Canadian way" either. We were, quite simply, doing things God's way, obeying His directives, not weighed down by conformity based on cultural expectations or identity.

We were even liberated on a personal level because, as I mentioned before, those who were familiar with us and our gifts had inadvertently squelched our calling by seeing us as who we *were* or who they perceived us to be, rather than as who we *are* in Christ. We were also more useful in this new environment given that, as "outsiders," we had a fresh vantage point. We were able to view things from a completely different perspective than those who had become accustomed to a potentially altered or skewed reality. That which had become commonplace to the natives of this country, were obvious areas of concern to those of us who were able to see this place or situation from a new and potentially clearer or untarnished perspective.

> It's possible in our countries of origin to become
> blinded and lose objectivity in relation to that which is
> ugly or wrong, only because it is all that we know.

It is also true that for those who have been called away from that which is familiar, there is a tendency to be far more diligent and consistent in seeking the Lord as to *why*. We were constantly seeking His face in an effort to walk out the call on our lives. The reason He had brought us to this new place was a force with which to be reckoned.

It saddens me to admit I prayed for Scotland more in a very short period of time than I had ever, over a lifetime, prayed for the country of my birth. Why is that? It's because Canada had become familiar. Its issues and problems faded into the background of my own life, my own dreams and my own circumstances.

Since we'd arrived in the United Kingdom, I was far more focused on seeing Scotland set free because I knew I had been sent for a purpose and my desire was to carry out that purpose. I had not only been called *to* something, but I had also been called *away* from something, motivating me to make certain that I'd realized my calling, whatever the role. Although there had been many a dark day, I grew to a place of embracing even the lows on this crazy roller coaster ride of faith.

It is here that we can celebrate a full circle moment. We have arrived at the very place where this journey began on the first day of that brand new year, not long after the passing of my Dad. Although that was a difficult time and while many more gruelling days followed, I'm so grateful I persevered because the rest of the story, which I'm about to share, is what made it all worthwhile!

Chapter 8

ACTIVE FAITH

Dreams and Visions

UNITED WITH NEW friends from other nations, who had also arrived in obedience, all filled with faith, possessing little of earthly value, but with steadfast hearts set to wholly serve and follow Jesus, was a complete blessing! Finally, after eight long, desert-like months in our new country, it seemed that God was moving, things were shifting and changing and we'd do well to fasten our seatbelts and ready ourselves for the ride of a lifetime. There was a clearly distinctive link between eight of us.

> We were four couples from four nations with
> a powerful connection and mandate beyond
> anything we could have imagined.

In sharing our stories, revelations and dreams with one another, it was plain to see we were a team. This was no ordinary team but something so completely God-created and God-ordained that it was like nothing I had ever seen or experienced. Representatives from Australia, Switzerland, Scotland and Canada had come together in the most remarkable of ways. We met with one another hoping to assemble the pieces of what turned out to be the most amazing, supernatural puzzle ever!

What we saw, once it was all laid out before us, was astounding. It was as though pictures and stories and directives literally came into full view. The more that we shared, met and prayed, the more we "saw." It was obvious our coming together was far from random chance. God had called each family to Inverness and although none of us could have predicted what He was doing or was about to do, we were thrilled to not only watch the plan unfold before us, but to actually be a part of that plan! He was establishing something brand new and we were honoured to participate. It was evident that we needed one another and we definitely needed daily instruction and wisdom from God in order to accomplish anything of lasting value. We were inspired, excited and relieved!

> I think one of the most stunning components
> of what transpired were the dreams.

We first connected at this level and in this way because of a dream and what followed was a string of God-inspired dreams all of which provided confirmation and information. Dreams became one of the key ways in which God communicated His plans with us and His warnings to us. It was wildly fascinating and utterly astonishing!

It wasn't long before God asked us to venture out of our warm, comfortable sharing meetings and "go." The first call was to the hills overlooking our city. A great deal of demonic and occult activity had and was taking place on these hills which is likely why the Lord wanted us there. We agreed to the assignment, viewing the experience as a celebration of His victory, knowing full well that the battle was the Lord's. Interestingly, we understood it to be a family affair and so the idea of identifying and tearing down demonic strongholds with children present was not going to happen, but then again, that wasn't what we'd been asked to do. We had been asked to go there and sing His praises, lifting up the name of Jesus.

> Our assignment was to declare Jesus as Lord from the
> high places, singing songs of worship, praying and
> breaking bread (taking communion) together.

We felt an urgency to complete this assignment in relatively short order and so we decided to coordinate with like-minded, worshiping warriors from Inverness and go to the hills the following week. It's a good thing we didn't wait any longer than the week, after seeing the amount of opposition by way of confusion, misunderstandings and a number of other personal and interpersonal "issues" that came our way. All were expected, but, truthfully, an annoying distraction. None of these things happened within the core group, rather amidst the on-lookers. We were determined to push through and past the distractions.

How glorious it is when there is strength in numbers and when joined with like-minded souls. As planned, we met together to pray before dividing up into five groups to climb five different hills, simultaneously. We got to the top of our respective hills, connected via cell phone and then, in unison and in unity, moved into a time of worship. Something amazing happened. God spoke to the children!!! Most of the panic and warnings from the on-lookers had been about the children and here we were on the hills, with the children being blessed by supernatural encounters with the Almighty!

This was just our introduction to another wild and crazy chapter in our journey with Jesus and the incredible blessings of serving alongside some of the most tuned-in, marvellous people we had ever met.

The week following our act of obedience was relatively quiet. We had a distinct sense that something in the spiritual realm had shifted and the witches and many others serving Satan in the region were very aware and angry about the ground that had been taken for Jesus. As expected, the enemy attempted to sweep in and discourage us but we stood strong, supporting and encouraging one another. It wasn't long before we were blessed with a week filled with dreams and visions like never before. The extraordinary part of this was that almost every dream, linked with another dream, answered questions and revealed critical information about the future.

One night I had a dream which left me hanging in anticipation for more, only to discover another member of our group had received a dream that completed mine! Not only that, but others had key dreams and visions that all tied in as well. There were even occasions when two people in the group had the same dream on the same night, but from different vantage points. Our appetite for God was growing stronger by the minute.

Over a period of less than a week, we shared about ten such dreams and visions along with other words, revelations and instructions that had been received. It was humbling and awe-inspiring to be a part of a move of God like this. We prayed together, read the Word and sought the Lord, clearly able to see we had been knit together according to the Spirit; it was imperative that we stay connected, in order to accomplish our part in what was intended for this place. In all honesty, that aspect of the "job" was extremely easy. These people were mature in their faith, in their ability to communicate effectively and highly skilled in their areas of expertise, so "working" together was, at every moment, a joy.

As the days and weeks passed, the four couples who had bonded in the most extraordinary of ways, continued to receive revelation through prayer, dreams, visions, prophetic words, and scripture. It wasn't long before we were called to step into even more. The battle was on and strangely, the very gifting and call that we'd been asked to lay down was precisely the one required for the task before us.

The worshiping warriors had been called into action!

The call to worship evangelism had, as it turned out, remained the call on our lives, but now it looked entirely different from anything we'd previously experienced. In this case it wasn't so much about seeing souls saved, although some were, but it was more about seeing the city set free from the many strongholds that sought to imprison its people in a state of blindness to the things of God. Our financial and musical resources were at an all time low. We couldn't fathom how we could accomplish the task before us with the limited number of musicians and "sponsors" in our midst.

After a brief battle with my desire for absolute excellence, I realized I needed to drop the old ways and just do what was being asked of us within the existing parameters. We needed to use what we had, use what had been provided; and what we had, was all of us!

It's ironic that I was desperately seeking a vocalist who could manage the songs and handle the warfare, rather than just stepping up and singing myself, but I think that the combination of having at long last released all things artistic combined with a dash of insecurity (assuming someone else could better fill this role) caused me to be wary of stepping up and stepping into that aspect of the calling. Regardless, the group of eight came together, pooling gifts and resources and wouldn't you know it, had everything and everyone needed in order to proceed.

Now for those of you who are surrounded by an abundance of people with finely tuned gifts, you need to understand the climate in which we were operating. There was very little music in the mainline churches. Well, let me clarify that. A large number of the churches were psalm-singing churches. If this is a new concept to you, it was also a new reality for us. Most of these churches only sang the psalms a cappella; no accompaniment, no band, no instruments of any kind. They didn't even use an organ! Because of this, there were very few Christian musicians to be found in the Highlands and even fewer with the required skill sets to "pull off" the mission before us. Generally speaking it seemed as though the level of the "bar" was quite low. I guess it stands to reason that if hopes and aspirations are clouded and oppressed, then aptitude and proficiency would follow suit.

Overcoming Obstacles

This brings us back to the spiritual state of Scotland, which, at the time, was actually quite bleak and in all honesty, shocking to the group of us foreigners. I don't want to paint an overtly negative picture, because obviously, like in all places, there is beauty and then there are the dark recesses, never captured in the pages of those lovely tourist brochures!

In reality, witchcraft and practices of the occult were accepted
as the norm and as part of the "culture."

Even Christians would inform me that this evil was simply
part of their heritage! One could walk past a shop and watch people
inside "playing" with a Ouija Board or see books and pamphlets on
ghosts and witches proudly displayed on the racks at the tourist
information centre. Entire districts in the city and even large
companies donned the name "druid." Houses built in these districts
or by these companies would be "decorated" with upside down
crosses, the sign of the devil. Folks openly walked about dressed
in full-length black capes, hoods up, white faces and black lipstick,
both men and women.

One particularly upsetting discovery was the meaning behind
the scads of cassette tape film we saw wound around the poles at
dangerous intersections. Apparently, occult members gathered
together and recorded curses into a tape recorder and then
proceeded to pull the tape out of the cassette and wrap it around
poles at these intersections, believing their curses would affect
the passing traffic. Interestingly, these intersections were in fact,
notorious for regular and bad accidents.

The degree of explicitly evil activity
was beyond comprehension.

We saw this first-hand when, after beginning the worship
evangelism at our original venue, the restaurant owners found a
tangled mess of cassette tape wrapped around their front door and
even around their parked car! Witches dropped in to make their
warnings known and threaten or just to "sit in" as we sang and
played. Interestingly they never stayed longer than a song or two!

It was disturbing, however, to know some of the local occult
members in the region were also still into human sacrifice! How
startling to come to the knowledge that the most likely reason the
United Kingdom has such a large number of missing persons, who
are never found, is because of these satanic practices! We were
shown houses with underground pathways to graveyards where all

sorts of demonic activity occurred on an ongoing basis and learned of more horrors than I care to share.

Working against this was, in a word, challenging. When faced with this opposition, I was reminded of a woman in Canada, saved by grace, who had previously been a self-proclaimed witch. Interestingly, this woman noted that, even while serving the devil, she was always very aware of the prayers of Christians. She expressed how frustrating it was for both her and the others in the coven, because when Christians prayed against their demonic activity in power, victory and authority, they needed to start the curses all over again! What we Christians can deal with in a heartbeat, took them a very long time to try and reverse.

> It's fascinating to note that even those who serve the devil recognize that God's power is greater. We need to remember this!

We ought to embrace and utilize the authority that's been given us. I must, however, interject a word of caution. Please be extremely careful when dealing with anything of this nature, making certain you are well equipped and have back-up! While we do walk in authority, I've found there seem to be different levels of authority, both within the enemy's camp and our own. If we really don't know what we're doing or if we're operating outside of our designated authority, we could get hurt. Only do that which the Father asks of you.

Another obstacle directly in our path was religiosity, something that might be seen as residing on the opposite end of the scale and yet wasn't. The wildly indoctrinated religious spirit found among so many of the church-goers was shocking. Laws, rules and regulations were the order of the day. One friend spoke of what it was like growing up in an environment such as this. She told us that children were not permitted to play on Sundays. Public playgrounds would be closed with the swings tied up and parents would remove all the toys in the house for fear of being excommunicated from the church if they hadn't properly observed the Sabbath. It was terrible. As a matter of fact, in certain areas of Scotland, this was still happening while we were there.

The religious spirit had literally driven people out of the churches and away from God. In fact, this religiosity was actually more unsettling than the demonic, because it was entirely more deceptive than the blatantly obvious Satanists. A religious spirit is, essentially, the demonic dressed up to look "pretty" and "safe" but is, in fact, yet another lie of the enemy. It was disconcerting to think of the number of people who faithfully attended these types of churches every Sunday, unaware of the deception. Following Jesus requires real commitment to Him and is not based around traditions and rules.

Many did not have relationship (with Jesus), they had religion (with an institution). We need to come to Jesus on our knees, repentant for our sins, with a sincere desire to follow Him. The repentance needs to be personal, sincere and from the heart, not something we are bullied into. It's all based on love and grace, not sin and condemnation. When the church becomes more committed to judging than it is to the love, grace and forgiveness found in Christ, it risks modelling an entirely flawed expression of our Lord and all that's encompassed by what He did at Calvary.

> We are required to love people – all people, regardless of their sins, opinions and even their religion, faith or lack thereof.

Again, what tends to happen is that the longer people are Christians they may become a little bit self-righteous, even to the place of pointing their fingers in judgment when telling people they need Jesus. Unfortunately, when this occurs, the "witness" is completely ineffective and even damaging, because it hasn't been executed in love. It puts us in the role of being the experts who have somehow "arrived" at some enchanted, idealistic destination, rather than the ordinary people we are, who are also on a journey and also in need of grace as much, or more, than the next guy. We don't need to pretend we have it all together, because we don't and others know that we don't. We aren't perfect, just saved, and that's thanks to Jesus.

It was also peculiar to observe that although the programs in most of these churches had become completely ineffective and their membership numbers had dwindled down to almost nothing, they refused to consider any other way of "doing or being church." What they couldn't seem to fathom was that the majority of unsaved people in the area had no interest whatsoever in attending church *period*. These people had no desire to hear what the church had to say.

The damage that had been done over the years was devastating. Doing things the same way would not work! Almost two generations had no real substantial experience with church, let alone with faith. Their parents and grandparents had experienced "the church" and had actually cautioned their children to stay away. The number of youth attending services was diminutive and disheartening. Broken homes were the norm and alcoholism, a serious problem. A lot of work needed to be done before people would even consider re-visiting the idea of a life of faith.

A severe lack of understanding, within the church, as to what it means to operate under the leading of the Holy Spirit, was another huge problem that we encountered. Our little group of believers, who were led both by the Scriptures and by the Holy Spirit, made this larger group very uncomfortable. They had become accustomed to certain ways of doing things and we didn't fit with their pre-conceived notions about serving God and ways in which to reach a completely lost, disinterested and even suspicious community. The non-believers of Scotland were not interested in religion nor were they going to be attracted to God via any man-made method or program.

> The power of the Holy Spirit would draw people, change
> people and transform Scotland.

Action!

It became painfully obvious that the best way to reach the lost was to go and spend time with them. We needed to hear what they had to say and not judge them. We needed to engage with them *without* an agenda. That's right; I believe in the Word and in evangelism, but we were required to just sit with folks, love them and trust that God would do the rest. By making ourselves accessible and available, we believed these folks would begin to see Christians and Christianity in a new light. We also knew they needed to see us regularly and consistently so they could come to rely on us. A healthy community is established in love and built on a foundation of trust!

It was time to act! We applied ourselves to the task at hand and, in no time at all, had located enough musicians to form a full gospel band, a venue in which to play, street evangelists, a prayer team, greeters, an administrator, a website designer and more. We realized that finding a restaurant or coffee shop that would remain open and allow us to do our "thing" might be a challenge, but we were determined. Thank the Lord, one agreed. It was situated amidst all the popular pubs and bars where people would congregate with a mission to drink until drunk. These were not nice, trendy pubs, but places that seemed to have no redeeming qualities whatsoever, causing us to, once again, marvel at the miserable state of affairs and people's acceptance of this reality.

The plan was for the band to provide professional gospel music (the word "professional" speaks to the level of the role and not to payment – which was nil). The street evangelists would mingle with people both inside and outside the venue, chatting with passers-by and answering any questions they had, while the prayer team prayed from within the coffee shop, outside on the streets or wherever led, depending on the direction and strategy given them by God each night.

We left the venue's door open all evening, so that the music could pour out into the streets and be released into the environment. In the beginning, it was rough going for all the team members, feeling as though we were slogging through a murky sludge about a mile high. But slog we did, pushing through and past all sorts of opposition and discouragement.

Even though there were difficult days, there were always
blessings to be found.

We didn't focus too heavily on advertising our events, given that our potential "audience" could be found right outside the venue door, roaming the streets. We notified a few of the recovery centres and missions, but primarily trusted the Lord to send those who were meant to attend.

As anticipated there were, indeed, people God had on His heart. In fact, there were quite a number of people who were drawn by the power of the Holy Spirit and connected with us in conversation or in response to the music. This is what made it all worthwhile. Some passers-by hovered at the door while others ventured inside and stayed for a coffee. Still others couldn't get enough of the joy and the peace that permeated the room and happily spent a large portion of their evening with us. It didn't take long to see that what we were doing was not only an encouragement to the lost, but also to the believers who desperately wanted to see change. The more they came out to listen or observe, the more they wanted to participate.

> As this type of evangelism was being modelled,
> those hungry to serve were quick to respond.

We could see a real boldness coming upon them. Without any prompting, they actively jumped out of their seats to welcome those who'd stopped by, generously purchasing coffees for strangers with money from their own pockets. Sometimes they donned their jackets and went outside to speak with people or prayed up and down the streets. It was exciting to see how infectious sharing the love of Jesus had become and equally interesting to note how much these Christians genuinely wanted to be involved in something that mattered. They had a fresh determination and renewed hope to see their city revived. One of our very first "Holy Spirit-drawn visitors" was a young man who had ventured away from his pub buddies to stop in and see what was happening in our venue.

He looked to be about twenty-years-old and truthfully, appeared a little confused as he ventured into the restaurant. He sat down at a table close to the band, settling in, unbeknownst to him, next to one of our daughters. There was something genuine about his interest in what was going on. He asked if he could look at the lyrics of our songs as we "performed." We pulled some music out of our binder for him and I could see my daughter (also a musician) helping him follow along.

It was near the end of the evening and although I had planned to speak with him, I became preoccupied with the business of a hurried clean-up. I glanced over and noticed others chatting with him so I carried on with the job at hand. After dropping off one of the final loads of equipment outside, I noticed our new young friend standing there alone, evidently struggling with his fleshly desire to leave but yet being held at bay by something bigger and stronger than himself. Against his natural inclination to run in the opposite direction, he allowed himself to become engaged in a conversation with me.

It didn't take long for me to discover he was mildly intoxicated and also furious with God. I stood and listened to him as he spouted obscenities and "let it all out." After a while he did calm down, at which point I was able to ask him why he was so angry with God. "He's letting my parents get divorced," was his quick reply. "Now my mom is all alone and I'm mad," he continued, but with that, his lip began to quiver. As he struggled to regain his composure, I asked if I could pray for him. I was surprised by his quick reply in the affirmative, followed by a bowed head. It was a fascinating dichotomy at play as we stood together in a "holy" moment, seeking the Lord God Almighty for His hand to touch this young man and his family, amidst drunken revellers, hooting and hollering all around us!

Our new friend became a "regular," stopping in to see us through-out the three months we were out on the streets. Interestingly, the Lord still brings him to mind quite often, along with a couple who only came by just once to see us. The man appeared unaffected but the woman was contemplative, teary-eyed and even seemed to sing along. We wondered if she was a believer from another community, but before we had the opportunity to speak with her, they left.

Prior to leaving, she scribbled a note and left it behind. In essence, the note said, "You may think that what you are doing isn't working, but it is and I thank you. I am lost. Please pray for me." Our hearts broke and we were, once again, reminded of why we had been called to this. There were other testimonies, too and each one inspired us and helped us to remain focused on the task at hand. So many stories … so many people … so many beautiful moments but still, it seemed to be a slow process.

> Then, after about six or seven weekends of worship on the streets, we sensed break-through!

This break-through coincided with a visit from a guest itinerant speaker who had brought a word for Scotland. Hosting this anointed preacher from Canada was both a blessing and a challenge. He had a connection with a ministry in North America that was completely unorthodox, giving new meaning to the expression, "out of the box." Even though he was in Scotland as a representative of his own ministry, as sent by God, we could see that this connection might create some problems in Scotland but not to the full extent of the havoc actually realized. The religious spirit was already being shaken so when this speaker arrived, the shaking seemed to increase to new heights. Regardless of this, for those of us who had been praying for change, it was a tremendous encouragement to know that without a shadow of a doubt, something hugely significant had and was occurring in the spiritual realm! Apparently, we and he had exhibited the tenacity and perseverance to follow through with our part, God had done His thing, which was the truly awesome part; now things were different. Transformation was taking place before our very eyes.

> God was completing the work He had begun and things were changing!

It was fascinating to see how this persistence in the town centre had altered the spiritual atmosphere. It wasn't just the work of our team but so many others too: street pastors, the healing-on-the-streets folks, missionaries, prayer warriors, prophetic treasure hunters and more, all of whom had fulfilled their calling, so that together we could rejoice as godly change came to the city.

Moving into a new venue was the next step for our team. With that move came an increased level of freedom and release. We welcomed the change and revelled in the love and acceptance we experienced in this new location.

It was around this same time one of our team members reminded us of a government program that had been initiated some time back. It was a campaign that focused on encouraging drinkers to take a break, clear their heads and enjoy a cup of coffee before moving on to their next watering hole. It was a decent enough initiative, but obviously hadn't been properly thought through, because until we'd come along, there hadn't actually been any coffee shops open for the sensible drinkers to adopt this idea!

Armed with a renewed sense of break-through along with some enlightening data, we became influencers in the political arena. We began by encouraging the members of the Scottish Parliament to drop in to see what we were doing and then took it a step further by challenging them to allocate some resources to this initiative.

> Thanks to the incredible favour of our Lord, we were able to
> stir these politicians and prompt them to take notice of not
> just the problems in their city but also the potential solutions.

Excessive drinking, a lack of activities and resources for young people to keep them free from this ingratiated evil, and the desperate need for healthy social activities, were all concerns. These problems needed to be addressed, and we believed that in "rewarding" the willing owners of these coffee shops who'd agreed to remain open, positive change would result. Our plight was, at long last, noticed. One Member of Scottish Parliament in particular came by to see us on a couple of occasions and not only did he listen to our thoughts and ideas, but he began to take some initiative. After he'd witnessed what was happening in the venue and saw the positive effect it was having, he became motivated to become a part of the solution.

> He had to admit that our small group from the nations had been able to initiate and see remarkable change come to the "culture" of the downtown core within a short period of time.

Of course, it was actually one small group, led by one very large God! By doing what we could with what we had, things had changed, in the people, in the spiritual and in the natural. The politician could see that our clientele was as varied as one could imagine: young and old, saved and unsaved, drinkers and teetotallers, locals and foreigners. But the truly outstanding element was that during our three months on the streets, the crime rate had dropped substantially! It spoke volumes about the impact of the Spirit and His vessels.

As lasting change was becoming a reality, God had shown us that our time in Scotland was coming to a close and we would be moving on. We needed to pass the torch on to those who would remain. It had been a ride unlike anything I'd ever experienced and now this particular chapter, for me and for us, was coming to a relatively speedy conclusion. There were so many thoughts and emotions, so much to reflect upon and so much to look forward to, as we considered what the future might hold. The reactions of our Scottish friends were as a single voice; they were despondent at our leaving. They had prayed passionately for years for those who would be sent from the nations. God had responded and now, it was the end of an era. It would be difficult for all of us to adjust. It had been a roller coaster fifteen months and now it was over. Our role and our assignment had been completed. We were leaving having seen a community changed, a people changed and we ourselves were leaving, changed, forever changed.

Perseverance

Seasons come and seasons go and through it all I've grown to see patterns in how God speaks to us, uses us and moves us. This is good. What's challenging is that I am now more quickly able to perceive when a dry or difficult season is approaching.

Although grateful to have grown in my ability to recognize these signs, it's also true that as a result of having "warred" through previous obstacles, valleys and worries, I seem to experience the onslaught of weariness and discouragement more swiftly. The things I was easily able to combat early in my walk—things that should have become easier with age—had actually become more difficult. With the passing of time, I found myself lacking the energy or the will to keep up the "fight." I had developed a very bad habit of saying (usually internally) things like, "I can't do this anymore" or "I'm done." Obviously these words were not bringing me to a place of break-through, but quite the opposite. At some point, I analyzed what I'd been saying and the more I thought about it, the more I had to question what I was actually "done" with. Was I done with God? No! Was I done with faith? No! In truth, I was done with the devil. I needed to change my words and my thoughts to line up with God.

Let's be resolute in our walk, determined to press on and through the trials that come with life and the persecutions that come with faith. It's all part of the journey. When Jesus healed the paralytic as described in Luke 5, He admired and honoured the perseverance of the men who had "gone the extra mile" to see to it that their friend would be healed. It took a great deal of effort and ingenuity to come up with the clever strategy to climb, bed and all, up to the top of the house and then execute that plan by lowering their friend and his bed, through the roof! Now that's tenacity at its finest. It is also a perfect example of what it is to bear one another's burdens and how our faith can be used to help support others.

I believe God longs for us to operate from a place of love and humility, so that in spite of our circumstances, position, finances or spiritual maturity, we might grow a right and generous heart for service. He wants us to know that we can begin to do things for the Kingdom right now with whatever we have. What's incredible is that no matter how insignificant our contribution may appear, He will bless it and increase the value beyond anything we could have imagined.

> We can't keep waiting for some magical day when everything or everyone will be in a perfect place or position before we step out of our own pain and begin to reach out to help another.

That "magical" day actually looks like *today*! If not, the day may never come, giving us reason, or an excuse, to never start. Sometimes people try to move directly into their "call" and then when it doesn't go smoothly they become discouraged and give up. If you've had a prophetic word spoken over you and it rings true and it's been confirmed, then boldly step into that call but keep in mind there are times when a number of steps may need to precede the fulfilment of that prophecy. You may need to do what you can, where you are. You may need to choose to serve in a lesser capacity in an environment where you hope to, one day, fulfil your calling.

Take, for example, a young college graduate whose desire it is to operate a business. While a formal education will greatly assist him in his plight, the more meaningful teaching will come from observing and speaking with those who are already successfully doing what he wants to do. As the "rookie" meets with these proficient business people, surrounding himself in the desired environment, doing whatever he can, he will not only learn important lessons and strategies but he will form and nurture relationships that will likely aid him in the future. He may need to volunteer to sharpen pencils and take out the trash at the beginning, but he'll be "serving" where he can, in an appropriate environment and through that action, God is able to use what he is doing to bless the activity and him!

We need to begin by doing our small part for the Kingdom and then watch God's wondrous plan unfold before our eyes as He adds the *super*natural onto what we have done in the natural. Now hear me when I say that I'm not advocating doing a bunch of meaningless stuff in a fleshly way, but to instead watch for opportunities in which God may wish to use us right where we are now! As we do what we are able, God will lead us and transform our efforts into something more wonderful than anything we could have accomplished in our own strength.

A very dear friend of mine in Scotland lived out this very principle. Back when she was a brand new Christian, she was propelled towards a desire to do her part for the Kingdom. She desperately wanted to serve God, but because she didn't possess much materially, and spiritually she was considered to be just a baby, she realized her contribution could appear modest. Regardless, determination won out and she continued to seek God and watch for opportunities to make a difference. One day, she read an ad for an organization that was looking for good, used children's clothing.

"This," she thought, "I can do!"

She was a woman on a mission. In no time at all, she had collected an impressive and weighty donation. She methodically and meticulously laundered, pressed and folded everything, grouping items together according to size and gender. She went "all out" and was eager to present this gift, thrilled at having found something she could accomplish that was within her means.

She jumped into her little car, full of precious treasures for those in need and off she went! She brought everything into the centre that had placed the ad, trembling with pleasure, at having been able to *do* something for God. However, the reception she received was far from what she'd expected or hoped. The woman collecting the goods didn't even thank her, but asked her why she had "gone to so much bother." My friend explained she was a Christian who wanted to give of herself for God. The woman's response was full of disdain, sneering "you do-gooder Christians are here today and gone tomorrow." With that, my friend (a brand new Christian) silently left the centre, unable to comprehend what had just happened.

After the initial shock wore off, she decided that she needed to demonstrate the love of God to this woman. She wanted her to know that Christians weren't as she'd described them to be, and even if unable to alter the woman's opinion, my friend was resolute in her decision to do this for God. With that, she continued to collect and bring items in on a regular basis. Churches in the area began to expect my friend to drop in frequently and regularly to pick up the clothing they were now collecting on her behalf.

One day, she received a rather remarkable gift. It was a stunning, deluxe model twin stroller. After much manoeuvring, my friend stuffed the fantastic find into her little vehicle, anxious to get to the centre, where she could reveal the beautiful stroller to the staff. As only God can orchestrate these things, she had no sooner pulled up to the centre and leapt out of the car when she ran smack dab into an extremely pregnant woman who was being told that the centre "rarely received strollers and had never been given a twin stroller." With that, my friend excitedly motioned the woman over to her car, revealing the gem in the back of her vehicle.

> She was amazed by what God had done and was doing,
> motivating her to an even greater level of service!

Not long after, while delivering a cot to another mom-to-be, my friend was shocked to find that this poor soul, who was nearly nine months pregnant, was living in a completely empty flat. There were a few blankets strewn on the floor where this sweet woman must have slept but other than that, she had nothing.

Apparently, she was a victim of domestic violence, who had escaped the clutches of her abusive partner and was literally in dire straits. My friend viewed this as an opportunity from God to give. So, she along with the support of a pastor and his congregation had, within a week, not only put the word out as to the need, but had successfully seen to it that this expectant mom's home was cleaned, painted, furnished and filled in good time for the arrival of the baby!

What happened next, my exceptional friend could never have anticipated, as gifts of furniture and other donated items continued to pour in, long after the initial need had been met. She didn't know what to do with so many things, mostly all large. She made some calls to see if she could locate a vacant warehouse and even sought out funding streams to cover the expenses associated with storage facilities.

When demand exceeded supply, God drew others who were doing a similar work together to form a partnership which ultimately resulted in the formation of new charity, reflected in what is now one of, if not *the*, largest growing charitable organization in all of Scotland! As a matter of fact, it was this company to whom we had given our large sofa, when we first arrived, long before meeting one of its founders! In having started where she was, with what she had, God was glorified. Her obedient, willing heart and actions had been blessed, moving both her and the activity well beyond her capacity and into one that could only be attributed to God.

> In order to move forward, it's imperative that we take our eyes off of ourselves and our own situations.

We need to remember we are here to be used by God. He has provided us with eyes to see the needs of those around us, arms to embrace the hurting and legs to walk alongside those who need a friend.

When we were in Scotland, an acquaintance from Europe, whom we had met in Canada, decided to come and spend time with us. We didn't know him very well and so while happy to see a familiar face, we were also a little surprised he had made the journey.

As we sat together in our tiny living room, I thought to myself, "okay this might be awkward." Our guest was far closer to Kevin than to me, and Kevin was busy that day and wouldn't be home for a number of hours. I was grateful to know that the kids would soon be home from school. Our guest was the first to break the silence, not with light and polite conversation but rather with deep, heartfelt, personal and highly traumatic experiences from his past. I was riveted and deeply moved.

He confessed he didn't know the reasons for his transparency, nor did he fully understand why he had made the trip, only that he had.

I surprised even myself with my speedy response. "I know why you're here. God sent you. He wants you to know how much He loves you so He sent you to us, so that we can assure you of this truth." Hearing and sensing the unconditional love of the Father was almost more than he could handle.

That week, like it or not, he was immersed in all that we were doing on the streets. Although it was completely foreign to him, it didn't take long before he got into the swing of things. Not only had God placed us in his life but as only God can orchestrate these things, one of our team members spoke his language meaning that there was someone close at hand who could answer his 'God' questions in his mother tongue! Amazing! The day before he left, he committed his life to Christ! How refreshing it was to care for the needs and struggles of another.

When we become too self-absorbed, we
also tend to become ineffective.

Again, by taking the focus off of our own problems and difficulties, we can be effective for the Kingdom and our troubles evaporate into the background of a work and a mission that matters to God. Over time we find ourselves caring more about the things of God, than being consumed by the things of "us." Let's be so in tune with God that whatever touches His heart, touches ours. This is what matters! If our hearts become entwined with God's, then we find ourselves caring about that which He cares about. When we move into this state of being, it's as though our relationship with our Lord and Saviour becomes a partnership, and that's mind-blowing.

Chapter 9

LIFE OF FAITH

Lessons Learned

THROUGHOUT THIS JOURNEY of faith I have learned many a valuable lesson. While in Scotland, we learned how to operate in biblical community. We not only shared our lives and our hearts with one another, but were blessed with the opportunity to care for one another in a way we had never previously experienced. It was all about manna for the day; it was not storing up for ourselves when we knew that our brother or sister down the road was in need today. The generosity amidst this group, none of whom had financial wealth of any kind, was staggering. It gave new meaning to the concept of "sacrificial giving" and "community living."

While it can be excruciatingly difficult to give when you, yourself are in need, it is beyond humbling to be on the receiving end of just such a gift. When someone gives out of lack, not out of abundance, it inspires. By the example modelled, we were motivated to look beyond our own state of affairs and consider the needs of others. If these people could give selflessly, then so could we. It astounded me as to how deeply our Heavenly Father loves and cares for us. At a time when we might have been wise to question our very sanity,

He connected us with friends walking a similar path,
allowing us the opportunity to edify,
support and build one another up in the faith.

Our God doesn't want, or deserve, to be put into a box. If we are willing and available, He will use us and although it's possible to become grieved by various trials, the genuineness of our faith is much more precious than gold and ultimately, at the end of faith, we receive the salvation of our souls. We receive much more than we could ever give. Still, we must give ourselves over to a Holy life, lived for God.

Our giving and serving should be purposeful and without bitterness or reserve for as Paul says, "God loves a cheerful giver."

When we give or serve in this fashion, we will reap bountifully. I learned this in a very obscure fashion.

One day as I rummaged through my purse in search of my keys, I realized I had lost my make-up bag. I was upset because I didn't have the money to replace the lost items and as a result of all my allergy/swelling issues, I desperately needed the help the make-up provided. Trust me, you know that old saying, "If the barn door needs painting, paint it!" And so, even after a friend offered to replace everything, I was still stewing about how stupid it was of me to have lost the bag.

Eventually my friend became frustrated with me and almost in exasperation, presented me with insight that caused a major paradigm shift in my thinking. He said, "You know, somebody else likely needed that more than you." Immediately, I was okay with it being gone and felt completely at peace. It put a whole new spin on cheerfully and purposefully giving as opposed to begrudgingly having had something removed or taken. Now, while the example may sound trite, the lesson isn't! Give generously, graciously and extravagantly, even when it seems as though you have little or nothing to offer; it is "the widow's mite." Change your perception about *having* to pay bills and taxes, loss of belongings or even having had something stolen. If we "give" and do so cheerfully, then God can and will bless us. This is not the world's way, but it is the way of God's economy.

I've learned to depend on God, knowing that He is my source in all things, in all ways and at all times. There is a very real responsibility given to those who possess much. They may think they deserve this wealth because they "worked for it" but this is wrong thinking. In the case of individuals and entire nations, all that we have, is due to God. He is the one who has provided each one of us with unique and wonderful opportunities, favour, wisdom and the ability to be gifted and blessed in the work that we do.

If God's favour were removed or illness were to strike us down or the market dramatically altered, or a natural disaster occurred, would any of us still possess all that we currently do? If there is any hesitation in agreeing with this principle, then please read the book of Job or look at the situation in Haiti following the earthquakes or examine the lives of those affected by the terrorist attacks of 9/11 (11/9 in other parts of the world!). Job had it all, until God removed His hand of blessing and allowed the enemy to wreak havoc with his life. It wasn't pretty. Humility is key and honouring God, necessary.

Of course, many of the godly who are blessed with abundance have often "done their parts" but that could also be said of Job or even of the poorest of the poor in a third world country. Hopefully we're all doing our best.

> When surrounded by more obstacles than opportunities
> or when God's hand of protection and provision is lifted,
> it really doesn't matter how much we "try."

All we have is because of Him and thanks to Him. In turn, that which we have is not ours to do with as we please. Just as the gifts of the Spirit are meant to edify and build up the body, so it is with finances that are not meant to be hoarded for our own gain. It's about selflessness. In dying to self, we recognize that our lives and our possessions aren't ours. Everything belongs to God.

Now, to be fair in all of this, let's take a moment to look at things from another perspective. What if those who currently live in lack were the ones with the riches? Would these people take the high road and bless others who required the help? If the tables were turned, would they bless those who once ignored them and their needs? Would they be giving and forgiving as Joseph was with his brothers? It's easy to criticize those who may appear to be our polar opposites, but we must look at our own hearts and recognize the frailty of our own condition. None of us is above sin.

Another particularly revelatory lesson on this journey was in relation to our systems and programs. These structures, often developed by churches, governments and other organizations are here to help and to guide. These groups provide services and functions that can be incredibly beneficial and can also serve as guideposts informing us as to our progress and perhaps even teaching us new ways in which to operate. Even so, they are not the be all and end all.

Our critics frequently voiced their concerns about us and, what they perceived to be, our blatant disregard for these structures. Because we aren't the ranting and raving, "Let's cause a dispute" type of people, this perception seemed very peculiar to us. We hadn't vocalized anything "politically" and were far from controversial, except perhaps by our actions in relation to our obedient steps. In the beginning, I allowed the judgments of others to negatively affect me, until I grew in wisdom and understanding.

Let's take, for example, something concrete like the school system. As it turns out, a number of people were convinced that our teenagers were going to be irreparably damaged by our "globe-trotting." They fretted that we hadn't fully considered the ramifications of what we were doing and were concerned that this life of faith of ours would somehow damage our kids. Ironically, those who kicked up a fuss were the Christians from our own age group while, in sharp contrast, younger Christians and unbelievers were drawn to the light and to the adventure. Now, specifically, in relation to the school system, the secular educators were also supportive and did not believe our children would be harmed. They could see the value in all they were learning through these life experiences and were not alarmed in the least.

God showed me these structures and institutions are generally a good thing. They only become bad when they don't work for an individual, a family or in a manner that permits folks to live in accordance with His will. If a child can't learn within the system, they need to be able to leave that system. If, in order to obey a call, one must work outside the system, then that is what must be done. I'm not speaking of lawlessness but of godliness.

> If we allow any program or system to dictate when and how or
> even what we do, then the system controls us and is no longer
> a help to us but a hindrance.

So, when all is said and done, I am not against the system, but I also won't allow it to control me. I serve God and not the system or the program. We knew when God wanted us to leave Canada for Scotland and we knew the timing of when we were to leave Scotland for Canada, neither of which suited the timelines of the school system. We chose to obey God. If God says to leave a country and it doesn't fit with the school's timetable, what do you do? Do you choose to obey God or do you allow the "system," which is there to guide and assist, dictate your walk?

This is not meant to be contentious, rather to encourage freedom! The same is true within the church. Sometimes the programs have a tendency to take on a life of their own, causing leaders to become so caught up in them, that it's nearly impossible to hear God's voice, let alone stop the run-away train in order to move in another direction, if led to do so. It's far more important to remain obedient and tuned in to our King, than it is to be so immersed in a program or idea that we become inflexible or unable to hear what is being said from on high.

Over the years we have also broadened our perspective on what it is to be members of the body of Christ. Although our family had left our homeland in obedience to a call, once settled, we became (as before) part of a larger body. We not only found fellowship with a small group, those from the nations, but also with a larger group.

The larger group was one that bore a recognizable church "title." Really though, both groups were "church," an assembly of believers. Both groups were made up of the body of Christ and both groups were God ordained and we loved being a part of both. Whether I am in Canada or Scotland or someplace else, I am still a part of the body of Christ.

Regardless of the name outside the building or the home where I fellowship, I have committed my life to Christ and am part of HIS church with a sincere and passionate desire to serve, learn, live, grow and worship Him among believers. I'd rather not get tied down by anything restrictive as I share what God was doing, so it is my hope that you will be able to catch the heart of what I am saying. While God did, indeed, move within the larger group, we observed something very fascinating about the magnitude of movement within the smaller group.

> The smaller group, the one comprised of folks from the nations, was more quickly and easily mobilized.

It wasn't encumbered by any processes or procedures of any kind. It was not only free to move but was also able to accomplish *much*! What God allowed our small group to do was to hear His voice clearly, without any limitations associated with religiosity, creeds, programs, directors, previous or current expectations, mission statements or "red tape." Because we weren't financially supported by a recognized organization or association, we didn't feel pressured to justify our moves and were void of the compelling need to build or create something just for the sake of busying ourselves with activities that might well be a good thing, but not necessarily a God thing. It became all about reading God's Word, hearing God's voice and obeying His directives.

We were still accountable to others so this wasn't anything contrary to God and His design, but likely contrary to how many have come to believe mission work or ministry should look. Again, please don't jump to the conclusion that I'm speaking of a mutiny away from the church, unless it is "religious," controlling or manipulative, in which case run far and fast. In fact, I love the church, because the church to me, is (I'll say it again) God's people. While it's true that many institutions are no longer effective, I would be wrong to make a blanket statement that would see me, inappropriately doing unto them, as they did unto me. So again, church is not about a building or an organization; it's about the body of Christ, not separated or compartmentalized by walls, doctrines or even by geographical lines.

> I would simply advise God's people to be solely bound to
> Christ rather than the organization, the plan or the program.

I often think of how the "religious" folk responded to Jesus. They weren't able to experience all that He had to offer, teach and do, primarily because they were too hung up on their rules and preconceived notions. As a matter of fact, Jesus performed very few miracles and taught very little in His homeland. He didn't spend much time trying to convince the learned He was the real deal. He simply went out and did what He was called to do, without their "approval."

Going Deeper

We are *all* the body of Christ and while one ministry may be smaller, without the same degree of structure doesn't speak to its validity or effectiveness. When God is in it, amazing things can and will happen regardless of all the surrounding parameters. When an organized body exhibits control rather than releasing its members to operate in His fullness, the results can be both disturbing and damaging. The intention is likely to make certain godly activity takes place, but in many cases, what results is a watered down gospel and a people who have lost their zeal, passion and readiness to serve.

As a result of the more controlling institutions, some people become disillusioned with serving at all. This is often because they have received false teaching. Sometimes this teaching claims that these folks either aren't "ready" or aren't "trained" enough to be effective. The mistake here is not only in what is being said, but in having listened to, and trusted people rather than God. Again, legalism, manipulation and control have the uncanny ability to suck the life and love out of people until they are left to sit lifeless and zombie-like in a misguided church building.

> We definitely need to be part of the body, but that doesn't mean we should be a part of denominationalism.

While in Scotland, there was a mini-revival of sorts. I don't even know if there is such a thing, but it's the only way I can describe what occurred in a tiny little village north of us. What happened over a very short period of time shook the religious spirit in a mighty way.

An evangelist was in town preaching the Gospel. The power of the Holy Spirit had drawn a number of lost, forgotten, "fringe-type" teenagers to one of the first meetings held by the visiting evangelist. These kids had not only shown up, but had, in complete and utter abandonment, enthusiastically turned their lives over to Christ. These youth were so fired up about the power of God that word spread quickly throughout the village.

A minister from a very traditional church in town decided to slip into one of the meetings to investigate what all the hoopla was about. His plan was to sit quietly at the back of the room and observe. God's plan was different. The minister became so overwhelmed by the powerful presence of the Holy Spirit that he stepped forward to receive prayer for healing.

Now picture this; a very traditional minister having the courage to come forward for prayer in a meeting, completely unfamiliar to him, when quite unexpectedly, a 'mob' of teens with piercings, strangely coloured hair and tattoos run towards him to lay hands on him and pray for him. This all took place before the evangelist could work his way through the crowd to pray for the minister himself. There was no need, though, because by the time the evangelist had made it there, the minister had already been healed by God, through the hands of these new believers who would have looked to the natural eye to be a somewhat motley crew.

You see, religion hadn't gotten a hold of these kids. They didn't know what the church saw as appropriate or inappropriate. All they had learned, in a few short days, was what Jesus did and so, as His followers, they simply went ahead and did what He did and God blessed it!

Over these years, all that we've accomplished and all that we've learned, the ultimate lessons have been the simplest; to love at all times, to die to self, to give and then give some more, and to pray, trust and obey.

> We seek God and then do whatever He tells us to do,
> when He tells us to do it … period!

I believe this is what church leaders should be doing, instead of trying to replicate what God has done or is doing someplace else or even imitating what has worked in the past. God's character remains the same, but what He asks of us changes and shifts with the seasons. I've worked with many professional artists and musicians. Some have made it their mission to "try" to be another (or better) Celine Dion, U2, One Direction or Michael W. Smith but they'll *never* do it. How can we ever be as good as, or better than, the real thing? It just won't happen.

I am always urging these artists to discover who they are and then do that really, really well. The same is true for churches. You needn't imitate or compete with another church that appears to have found success. Instead, be successful in whatever God has made you to be. Seek God, giving Him free reign in you and in your "church" to do as *He* pleases. Then, watch in awe and wonder as God begins to move, setting in motion a succession of events and blessings beyond your wildest dreams.

Another associated revelation came when we'd initially arrived in Scotland and discovered that so much of what God was asking of us was unrelated to our usual areas of giftedness, passion and interest. We grew to understand that we are much more than our gifts and our abilities.

At first, He was clearly using us but in a manner entirely different than ever before. Although difficult to comprehend, and at times almost impossible to live with, we realized that, yet again, God had provided us with a gift. We had been presented with the occasion to realize our Kingdom value, minus the skill-sets that had previously given us worth and value. When armed with little more than "us," we could see that, although stripped of everything we had once known or done or been, we could still be used. We could still be loved by the body and by our Saviour, not so much for what we could offer, but for who we were.

This stunning discovery helped us to empathize with those who incorrectly deem their gifts as being "lesser" than gifts possessed by others. Because we were not able to use ours, we began to feel useless, *but* we're not useless. No one is useless.

A good friend was preaching on this very subject one Sunday and illustrated his point by carrying an adorable baby boy to the front of the church. He asked the congregation what the infant was able to bring to the table? What was he able to offer? What was his "value" economically? Of course, from that perspective, this little one receives far more than he gives, but we were able to see that in God's economy, this little one held great value.

> I've learned that because we can become so engrossed in our gifts and talents, they can actually become a stumbling block as much as they can be an effective tool for Kingdom work.

While it's right and good to discover, grow and develop our gifts, we mustn't receive our sense of value from them. When too wrapped up in what we see as our "areas" of strength, it can prove harmful as we potentially block God from being able to use us in other ways.

I recognize this means moving w-a-a-a-ay outside our comfort zones. It stretches us into places where we don't want to be stretched, but this is perhaps where God wants us stretched. Having found ourselves in a place where virtually nothing was familiar, we needed to trust in God and be willing to allow Him to mould us at a time in our lives when one would think the majority of the moulding had already been done. Obviously, God wasn't finished with us.

For the first time in decades, I was able to view myself simply as one of the King's kids; not as a singer, concert promoter, event director, marketing manager, communications specialist, wife, mom, daughter, sister, grandma, mentor, friend, encourager, counsellor, company owner, chauffeur for the youth or any of the other things I'd been known to *do*, but rather as a real live woman with a heart for God and for His people, longing to serve Him in whatever capacity He chose. Was it difficult at first? Absolutely! So much of who we believe we are is wrapped up in our designated title or simply as others perceive us to be (based primarily on what we do), and not so much on the real live person inside – who breathes, laughs, cries and hurts just like everyone else. Although a trying process, it was well worth undergoing. I would speculate this is likely the same principle as that of the rich young ruler who was unable to give up his possessions to fully serve God.

> Perhaps many of us are unwilling to give up our gifts
> or whatever it is that might be dear to
> us, in order to serve God.

What a revolutionary thought! How could it be possible that God would ask us to lay down our gifts? I guess it's no different than Him asking the rich young ruler to give up His money (also a gift of God). Discover who you are without the stuff, the title, the family, the job, the ministry, the past, or whatever it is (good or bad) that may define you? I would encourage you to unearth who you are in Christ, if these things, talents, people or history weren't in your life.

Now, don't go and do anything crazy and say I told you to leave your church, job or spouse, because that is *not* what I'm saying. It would, however, be good if you could embark on an exploratory journey to find out who you are in Christ when emptied of all that has previously dictated that for you. I remember a business associate of mine who had absolutely beautiful long black hair, something she considered to be her greatest attribute. Sadly, there came a time when she required treatment for cancer and her hair began to fall out. Imagine losing the very thing that provides you with self-esteem. It was heart-wrenching to watch and yet, while devastating, it was also a gift to view herself and her beauty without the hair.

Consider the depression of 1929. As the stock market crashed, my guess is that the folks jumping out of the high rise buildings to their deaths were those who had lost a significant amount of money and couldn't imagine how they would ever function in this world without that "security." Those who'd never had much, shrugged their shoulders, fixed their eyes and hearts on the task before them and prepared themselves for another difficult season. It was those who were defined by what they had, who didn't know how to function without it, who decided to end it all. Now you might be thinking "yes, well money isn't all that important to me, so I wouldn't do that." Fair enough, then think of something that is and maybe you'll appreciate how those folks felt.

I didn't even realize what singing meant to me until I wasn't able. I also couldn't fathom a life without art and culture and yet, I've done just that. I'd always been the one to transport folks around (especially the young people) and then I found myself in the position of being the one who needed to receive the rides. I didn't realize the value of a somewhat prestigious career history, until I was in a new country and it held little to no power or influence.

What if we lost a limb, our sight, our hearing, or worse yet, a child, are we still useful in God's kingdom? Of course we are!! My "losses" seem small in comparison, but whatever it is you might be asked to sacrifice, whatever may have been stripped away, whatever has turned your world upside down, who are you? Finding oneself in this place has the potential to knock you right off your feet, but I would encourage you to remain steadfast, knowing Jesus will never leave you or forsake you.

He is growing our character and will continue to do so regardless of how uncomfortable or inconvenient it may be to us.

This is because He desires to bring us into His fullness and our destiny. I was speaking with a Christian radio announcer one day about some of the overtly nasty letters and emails he had received over some fairly trite issues. I asked him how he handled that sort of persecution day in and day out. He replied by saying that there were just as many letters of adoration and he had also learned to ignore those.

You see, if he listened to the naysayers, he would have called it quits long before. If he listened to his adoring fans, he would have thought himself to be something pretty fantastic, maybe even invincible. He realized that neither was truth. God's truth is where it's at! And so, we seek for revelation of God's truth in each and every circumstance. We desire to know what it is that He is trying to teach us. We pray with a sincere heart to be set free from all that is not God. We ask Him how He wants us to respond and who He wants us to become, and then, with discerning hearts, we forge ahead on this journey of faith.

Life of Faith

When we arrived in the U.K., we had no idea why God had called us there. People still ask us if we can sum it up in a sentence and we need to answer them with a simple "No, but if you have a few hours, we'd love to share our story." There's no way to encapsulate all the reasons for such an experience into a one-liner. So much happened to us individually, as a family and also, through us.

I love how God multi-tasks!

When in Scotland, we were honoured and humbled to discover God had answered many a prayer through us! Some of the bigger prayers, like those associated with the generational issues, the need for spiritual break-through in the land and its subsequent effects on our own country were, perhaps, more evident, but there were other prayers answered, too. Many of the young people we were privileged to meet, had prayed for years that God would send them Christian friends, and our teenage kids had become an answer to their prayers.

One exceptional sixteen-year-old had prayed for three years, that he would be able to play in a youth band. When we arrived and saw there was nothing of the sort, I formed one! This young lad is grown and currently studying music and technology at university while another member of that band continued to play with the "adult" group in the coffee shop that we left behind. From what I understand, there has been a breakthrough, not only spiritually, but also musically, in the area! Praise God!

For others, it was quite simply the boost and the encouragement they needed to carry on, pushing through and past the obstacles before them. Folks frequently told us that because of our act of obedience, our having modelled faith, evangelism and perseverance, their prayers had been answered.

Of course, we also received many answers to prayer ourselves in having been cared for daily; we were fed, clothed, sheltered and encouraged. We had been united with others who were also walking by faith. This was something we had longed to experience and was a blessing like none other. Not only were we able to see God at work, first-hand but we had also been delivered from an environment of accusations, bitterness and gossip by having been sent away. We were returning to our homeland as new and different people knowing God had touched us, and so had Scotland. Our hearts had become one with that faithful few who were passionate about seeing their nation turn to Christ. The experience had been filled with highs and lows like never before. We were leaving this land immersed in a "high." It was a time when we would have loved to stay, reminding us yet again,

our lives are not our own. We belong to
Christ and so we go where led.

Prior to returning to Canada, we had a very strong sense about a potential move to Australia. Initially, we thought we were to move "down under" right away, but that was not to be. Although we were looking forward to reconnecting with family and friends in Canada, we were disappointed when revelation came that Australia was "not yet." So, in obedience, we moved to British Columbia as led - the very place we'd considered moving prior to being sent to Scotland. It was quite something to behold, acknowledging that our "feelings" about British Columbia weren't wrong, just intended for another time – a time such as this!

Upon our arrival in British Columbia, we were faced with the stark reality that once again, we needed to start all over. Having packed just one suitcase and one carry-on each before leaving Scotland, we had no idea it would be almost a year and a half later before we would set eyes on the rest of our belongings, which had been whittled down to less than a third of what we'd brought to the U.K., and that was half of what we'd owned in the first place! So here we were, yet again, with no furniture, bedding, towels, dishes or cutlery, moving into yet another home in another new city with nothing but a few clothes. I must say, though, it was the quickest and easiest moving day ever! We rolled our suitcases in, brushed our hands together in approval of our accomplishment and said, "Whew ... that's it; everything's in!" Because we'd already experienced this, we knew how to cope and we also knew God would provide just as He had in the past, and He did.

The blessing throughout this season was in having garnered a powerful "history" with God, and a testimony of trust. We were also forever grateful to be in a community only a short distance from friends and a few miles from my mom. This was all really good! Still, I made one very significant error. I had the impression that once home and settled into life in Canada, things would be easier and that the trials associated with this faith walk would be a distant memory. This was not so. Again, another death was required and although intensely painful, I observed that the timeframe was shorter than the previous "death" which, in turn, was shorter than the one before that.

"It was our daughter's 17ᵗʰ birthday. Something deep inside of me began to hurt. Another "celebration" was upon us. It was another milestone to hold dear and another occasion in which we'd be reminded we had no gifts to give, no party to throw, no camera to capture those precious memories. I desperately wanted to do something special for her but it was out of our hands. We managed to scrape together some funds for a cake, invited a couple of girls over from down the street and "partied." Of course, we had no furniture and no dishes so we gathered around the island in the kitchen and made the most of what we had. Another piece of me died that day.

Thank God for kids who aren't all about the "stuff"; kids who choose to laugh and love in the difficult days, kids who are able to amuse themselves, creatively. Still, this was not how I'd envisioned commemorating her special day. Even so, I knew there were mothers out there, who would have given anything just to share a moment like this with their children – perhaps one never born, estranged, or passed. We were here and we were together and so I dug down deep and found genuine joy.

Growing in faith had obviously grown on me and in me and so, while I don't wish to diminish the anguish endured, it was encouraging to see I had become stronger in the Lord, with a larger capacity than ever before.

On a less personal note, I was also able to see my own country in a new light and was acutely aware of and disappointed by, the pervading indifference to faith. It seemed as though many were apathetic in their walks, having lost their enthusiasm to follow Jesus wholly, fully and without reserve. Although Scotland had its problems, still, there was a deep spiritual awareness, albeit misguided, but at least it could be found. North Americans, it seemed, had fallen into a slumber. I wanted to jump up and down and shake people, crying,

"Wake up! Wake up! We need to get mobilized!"

As we begin to operate in His power and not in our own strength, we can and will make a true and lasting difference in this world. We need to shake off fear and complacency, recognizing that, oftentimes, the only thing that's holding us back is us! I would urge you to awaken to these truths sooner, rather than later, knowing time is short. Grow in faith now. Do it before the inevitable – that day when He will separate the wheat from the chaff! Don't allow the things of this world to hinder your walk, but see obstacles and difficulties as mechanisms or springboards for growing in faith and character. We mustn't get bogged down by the things of this world.

> We are moving into a new age of God's dealings with mankind.

In order to catch this move, folks need to receive revelation that we are leaving this age behind. If we don't shift with the times, we won't have the effectiveness in Kingdom work that we desire. It's at times like these that mission statements don't bode well for us. They can cause us to become mired in the past, as we hold tightly to the incorrect assumption that nothing has changed. We may see ourselves as being "leading edge" because at one time, we were, but if we're not careful, we'll miss out on all the new things that God is doing. If we become set in our ways, we end up obsolete like many of those who have gone before. None of us want that. Let's catch this new wave and ride it with finesse, passion and prayer.

> Regardless of the cost, we need to align ourselves with all that God is saying and doing *now*.

It's easy to see how Britain, having had so many years to accumulate layers upon layers of enemy strongholds, has suffered. It's also a crucial lesson to those of us in younger nations. We need to sit up and take notice to ensure that history not repeat itself here. We must be vigilant and aware, ever and always praying and interceding for our communities, cities and countries. Let's prayerfully commit our way to the Lord, pursuing Him and His merciful grace so that we, and our nation, maintain the status of being a God fearing, God loving, God serving country.

It also needs to be said that although the enemy has attempted to create chaos in the U.K., we can also see that they have years and years of a rich spiritual heritage from which to draw! The Scots can hold tightly to God's promises, the prayers of those who have gone before and God's covenant through Jesus. When you stop and think about that, it's exhilarating to consider what will happen when freedom and revival come!

Romans 8:31a says, "If God is for us, who can be against us." I love this scripture, but for now, I'd ask you to consider the possibility that the Lord might be asking

Are *you for* Me or *against* Me?!

Now, more than ever before, we need to make very clear, succinct decisions. There is no room or time to sit on the fence. He will separate the sheep from the goats and when this occurs, it will be clearly evident who has been obedient and who hasn't. It will be obvious who has faith and who doesn't. If I have learned anything over all these years and through all these trials, it is to be obedient.

Obedience

In essence the faith walk is, once all is said and done, about being obedient. It comes down to a concept as simple as that! This obedience won't look the same tomorrow or in a week or in a year, depending on what God asks of us. Nor will my obedience necessarily look the same as yours. The Creator is far too creative to work like that!! Like I've said, different things are asked of us at different times, and different people are called to different things. "To everything there is a season, a time for every purpose under heaven" (Ecclesiastes 3:1).

In the end, it's about developing a close enough relationship with our Lord and Saviour, that when we hear His voice, we know it. So that when something is required of us, be it small or large, we obey and we follow. Interestingly in the Hebrew language, the words "hearing" and "obedience" are synonymous.

If we are immersed in prayer, spending time with the Lord and in the Word of God then, when we hear a request or a command, we will know it lines up with scripture and obedience will easily follow. Despite the years and times I have felt alone in this walk, God has taught me to graciously love those who don't understand, and He has at all times provided me with true friends. "Rejoice with those who rejoice, and weep with those who weep" (Romans 12:15).

It's true that in following Him, there will be hardships but along with these hardships comes refining. The process of refinement, though painful, is a necessary step in our growth. Our youngest child frequently experienced terrible growing pains. We tried our best to soothe her aching legs with warm baths and massages, but it was awful to watch her writhe in pain. I was unable to stop the hurting because she needed to grow. It was part of the process. I've heard it said that

> God loves us just the way we are but He also loves us too
> much to leave us this way!

It's because His love for us is all-encompassing that He takes us deeper. He's interested in growing and refining that which is of value to Him, and that would be us! Scripture says that God "will sit as a refiner and a purifier of silver" Malachi 3:3. To be refined, means we must allow ourselves to be placed into the hottest part of the flame. This not only sounds like agony, it is! But God doesn't simply walk away and leave us to "burn" in anguish but watches over us until the purification process is complete. When that occurs, He is able to see His own image reflected back to Him, in us. How absolutely glorious is that?! I trust this is what God is doing in my life. Although I know His work within me is ongoing, I see a light at the end of the proverbial tunnel. There's an ocean of opportunities before me. There are hundreds of thousands of people who don't yet know the love of Christ and I stand in faith, believing that I am being moulded into a worthy, useful vessel to be used more and more for His purposes to reveal His glory.

Refined, purified, sanctified … we stand ready. Ready to commit ourselves fully to Christ and to the calling that is on our lives; ready to live a life of significance and purpose. I don't want to simply exist here on this earth.

> I want to know that while Christ has made a difference *in* me,
> He's also made a difference *through* me.

This may mean experiencing some discomfort, rejection and pain. It may mean going against "the flow" but in the end, it's just as Mother Theresa said, it's between me and God. He is the one I aim to please. He is the one I trust. Even since I started sharing this walk of faith with you, I have learned to trust the Lord at a much deeper level. I've seen His loving hand, teaching, guiding, protecting and providing. Deep down, I thought there would come a day when His grace, patience and love would be stretched to the limit and He'd become weary of me, but He hasn't. He's shown me that *until* I trust Him with absolutely *everything* at *all times* and in *all ways*, He is unable to entrust me with the next assignment. And so it goes, I trust in faith, He is faithful and my faith grows.

> Even when looking at worldly success,
> those who rank among the most successful
> are also usually those who have failed the most.

It often takes a number of attempts before we get it right. If we don't grow from our errors, then they end up becoming a succession of failures that discourage and defeat us. However, if we take something valuable away from each blunder and choose to learn from our failures, then they aren't failures but lessons on the road to success. The difference between those of us who know God and those who don't, is that we have a Heavenly Father who is leading us every step of the way and He is incredibly patient and loving. If I stumble and fall, it is He who picks me up and holds me up, so I can dust myself off and endeavour to move on.

"Forgetting those things which are behind and reaching
forward to those things which are ahead, I press toward the
goal for the prize of the upward call of God in Christ Jesus."
—Philippians 3:13a, 14

In having been required to trust Him, with boldness and what might seem to be, an extreme measure of faith, it has allowed me to see beyond that which is customary or in keeping with tradition. I hope and pray that you will be inspired to hunger for a deeper, more meaningful relationship with Jesus. He really is able to accomplish all that concerns you today. I would encourage you to have faith, be strong, of good courage, and obedient to a call that will surely bring you into an adventure in faith! There's no life like it and the dividends are everlasting! It is worth the cost.

The merry-go-round is absolutely fine but the roller coaster is where it's at! I pray that you and I will receive whatever power the Holy Spirit will give, so that we can fully, completely and powerfully live for Him. God is not finished with me and He's not finished with you. I encourage you to choose Christ. Choose life. Choose faith. Don't fret about the past. Receive forgiveness and make the rest of your days count, knowing that if God is for you, then who can be against you. And, if you are *for* Him, then you are safely nestled in the arms of the Father of lights, who at the end of time will wipe away every tear with a guarantee of no more death, sorrow or pain.

Let's stand together, shoulder to shoulder, living with passion and love, fully surrendered to serving Christ in all ways and at all times, so that when we come to the end of our days here on earth, we will be able to say as Paul did:

"I have fought the good fight, I have finished
the race, I have kept the faith."
—2 Timothy 4:7

And we, in turn, will hopefully hear those long awaited words, "Well done, good and faithful servant."

Lovingly Dedicated To:

The extraordinary memory of a faithful and courageous man,
A loving and compassionate father
who fought the good fight and kept the faith.

And to my mother,
A strong and beautiful person who never ceased
to believe in me, even when forsaken by so many others.

I am also forever grateful to my husband and our four kids who lived and walked this faith journey together with me. I love you all more than words could ever say!

For more information: www.artsworkinternational.com

Appendix I

THE GOSPEL ... A LOVE STORY

It's not what you've done, good or bad.
It's about what HE's done to make it right and you righteous.

WHEN I THOUGHT of those readers who may not know or walk closely with Christ, I felt that this appendix could be helpful in bringing greater understanding. From my own experience, I remember being grilled by a news reporter who wanted to know my thoughts on how folks may or may not end up in hell. He persisted in "interrogating" me about this issue, firing questions at me, making one attempt after another to back me into a corner, apparently hoping to entice me to say something controversial that would make a good headline. Here I was trying to put on a beautiful, godly celebration and all that the journalist could focus on was trying to coerce me into saying something negative about my faith.

I quietly prayed, asking God for guidance and then responded with, "The only way to the Father is through His Son, Jesus Christ." I wasn't interested in getting bogged down by theology and divisive arguments. I knew I needed to redirect his focus from hell and damnation to the good news part of the story, which after repeating the same answer over and over again, I was finally able to accomplish. In actual fact, the real story *is* about the *love* of God and not what many see as the wrath of God.

> "For God did not send His Son into the world to condemn the world, but that the world through Him might be saved."
> —John 3:17

Many prefer to focus on hell but from what I have learned, hell was never intended for people, it was created for the devil and his angels (Matt. 25:41). It was only because of the sin of Adam and Eve that hell became an option for mankind. If we don't receive the gift of Salvation through Christ, *we* have chosen the alternative. The choice is ours.

Again, God takes all the flack for this, but in actuality, by rejecting the good news, it's we who have opted out of grace, favour and love. I realize this will likely upset some folks, but that's because it's uncomfortable to be faced with the fact that there are consequences for our actions or inactions. There is no sitting on the fence with God. He is gracious and long suffering, but once we've heard the story of His great love for us, then we need to make a decision.

> "For the wages of sin is death but the gift of God is eternal life in Christ Jesus our Lord."
> —Romans 6:23

We have all sinned and fall short of His glory and yet He offers us this amazing and unmerited gift. Although we keep messing up, He just keeps on loving us, so much in fact that He sent His only Son to become a curse on the cross, in order that we might be saved. We just need to say "yes" in faith and in obedience to the One who provided us with this extravagant gift. We *can* be saved thanks to God's grace, and our commitment to follow Jesus.

If you haven't yet made a decision to follow Jesus, I would strongly encourage you to get whatever answers you require in order to make this commitment. God promises that if we seek, we will find. Keep seeking the truth and you will find it and I assure you that when you find the truth, you will have found Christ.

That said, I do feel compelled to offer up a caution. If you are seeking, don't linger too long in making this decision. Simply put, we don't know when our days here on earth will be over and it's critically important that we live out our days and years with an absolute certainty that we will spend eternity with Jesus. It's more than okay to sincerely ask God to reveal Himself to you, but once He has made Himself real to you, don't delay in turning your life over to Him. The enemy would love to see us engulfed in the academia of it all when, in the end, what's required of us, is child-like faith.

> "Assuredly, I say to you, unless you are converted
> and become as little children, you will by no
> means enter the kingdom of heaven."
> —Matthew 18:3

We needn't complicate this. Jesus didn't come to condemn, but to save. He desires that none should perish and that we would all receive salvation. He loves us so much He sacrificed His own son for us. If you are ready to make a decision and would like to know and follow Jesus Christ, you need only acknowledge that you believe Jesus lived and died and rose again; that He is the Son of God and that you want to live your life for Him. Ask God to forgive you of your sins, to cleanse you, heal you and to release you from all that would hinder you from living a life of freedom. Invite Him to reign in your heart and pray that He protect you from all that's not Him. It's as simple as that. If you do this, then you will *know* that you have begun an incredible journey ... following our Lord and Saviour, Jesus Christ!!

If you made this decision today, allow me to be the first to welcome you into the family of God! While the walk won't always be easy, you will absolutely never ever regret having made this decision. Celebrate and experience the joy of the Lord to the fullest! Continue to walk with Him all the days of your life and you will spend eternity in His presence. How radical is that? We serve an amazing God and now you are a member of the body of Christ! This is not the end, but simply the beginning.

You will need to get your hands on a Bible and start the process of uncovering the truths and lessons found in God's word. The most recommended chapter of the Bible for new believers is the book of "John," the fourth book of the New Testament, so that's a great place to start. Then, as you grow in knowledge and understanding, you'll be motivated to go out and make disciples of others, encouraging them to be followers of Jesus, too. Get connected to other believers and also learn about water baptism and the baptism of the Holy Spirit. Congratulations on the best decision of your life!

Appendix II

THE "SONS OF THUNDER"

DREAMS/VISIONS, BY JAMES RYLE

A Synopsis of Dreams by James Ryle

THE FOLLOWING INSIGHT occurred to me in August 1990 as a result of three dreams. In the *first dream* I saw a flatbed trailer with a curtain behind it. This trailer was parked at a fairground, as if a concert was about to happen. There were two guitars on the mobile stage. The color of these guitars was the most vivid, electric blue that one could imagine. What impressed me most was that the guitars were not painted, but stained. It had obviously taken time to make them blue. The curtain was the same color as the guitars.

Two men walked from behind the curtain with sheet music in their hands. They were very excited, and could hardly wait to play this music. One said to the other, "Wait till they hear this. It's going to be just like when the Beatles played their music!"

In the dream I also became excited. I turned to see the crowd gathering at the stage and the scene changed before my eyes. The audience became a vast body of water, like a lake, and as the musicians played the new song I saw fishing lines cast out into the water. The dream ended. My waking thoughts were that God is about to release a new kind of song in the streets. It will bring a revelation of the truth and it will usher people into His presence.

The anointing of the Lord will be with musicians who have spent time in God's presence "behind the curtain" receiving a deep love for the lost. The lyrics of their songs will be as "fishing lines" cast into the hearts of men and women needing Christ.

In the *second dream*, I was on the stage in a large church. There was an equipment room on the right side of the stage. It had microphones, cables, amplifiers and other kinds of things that collect in closets. In one corner of the room I saw a power amplifier covered with dust. The cord was wrapped about it, and it had not been used for a long time.

When I looked closer I saw written on the front, "The Beatles Power Amp." I knew in that moment that this box was the source of their sound and their power. I knew that anyone could plug into this box and, in effect, have what the Beatles had - an incredible ability to mobilize masses of people to a single thing.

As I stood there holding the Beatles power amplifier, I asked aloud this question, "What is this doing here in the church's equipment room?" Suddenly I was out of the equipment room and standing behind the pulpit at this church, still holding the amp. The enormous church, throughout the main floor and all about the balcony, was packed with people from every nation. A very beautiful woman, radiant with a glow of glory, stood in the middle of the church and began singing a song from the Lord. A light shone upon her and her voice filled the auditorium. All she sang was, "In the name of Jesus Christ the Lord we say unto you, be saved." She sang it over and over. She would turn to her right and sing, then turn to her left and sing; then she would turn behind her and before her and sing the same thing. As I watched her sing, it was like a wind blowing on a wheat field. The people began to swoon in the presence of God and then collapse in their seats, converted to Christ! God's power was moving through the music. The dream ended.

My thoughts upon waking were clear. There is going to be a new sound and distinctive anointing from the Lord upon music that will turn the heads and capture the hearts of men and women for Jesus. The reason the Beatles power Amp was in the church's equipment room is because God meant for it to be a part of the church's equipment in reaching the lost for Christ.

Music does not belong to the world, but to the Church. Music does not belong to the Devil, but to Christ. Satan has indeed stolen the hearts of musicians and their gift of music to use for his own evil purposes. The Church in many cases has unwittingly surrendered this to the devil without any fight at all. Music was given to worship the Lord but Satan has turned it for self-worship, which is the reason people tend to worship musicians. But true worship and true music belong to Jesus Christ. They are given to His church to serve Him with.

I truly believe the anointing the Lord will release on music is going to sweep the world in a manner like the Beatles did when they first performed. But instead of drawing attention to themselves (like the Beatles did), the anointed musicians of the Lord will draw attention to Christ alone and give Him all the glory.

In the *third dream* I was again in the large church where I had seen the amplifier. This time the church was empty except for one man. He was up on stage playing a keyboard and singing to the Lord. It was a beautiful song, and he was crying because of the tender exchange taking place between he and Jesus. He was writing the song right there, spontaneously making it up as he went. I was greatly moved by this song and the man's pure worship.

I had a camera with me and decided to take a picture of this to remember it. I took two Polaroid pictures that came out immediately. When I looked at these pictures I was stunned because both of them were glowing with a golden light. I looked up and then I could see it on the man. The entire platform around him was also glowing like gold. I knew that this was the anointing of God. I showed the man, but it startled him. He looked at the pictures for a second, putting his hands in his pockets he shrugged his shoulders and kicked the ground shyly, "Gosh, I didn't know you were here, I'm so embarrassed" was all he could say.

"You don't have to apologize for the anointing" I replied. The dream changed. I still had the two photographs of the anointed worshiper in one hand, and in the other I held a parchment. I looked at the scroll and saw it was a letter written by an unknown soldier in the Salvation Army. It said, "The Lord will release into the streets an army of worshiping warriors known as the Sons of Thunder. They will bring forth a witness of worship and praise for the Lord Jesus Christ that will bring many people to God."

The dream changed once more. I was floating over a wide and long highway that headed in one direction. All lanes were completely grid-locked, jam packed with motorcycle gang members, revving their engines and stirring up dust. It was a graphic picture of lost humanity. Then I saw a group of bikers moving in single file along the service road. They were headed for a field in the distance where there was a monolithic stone. This stone, I knew in the dream, represented the power of Christ and would empower those who touched it to go back to the highway and turn masses of lost people back to God. I looked closer at these motorcyclists as they sped toward the Stone, and saw on their jackets the words "Sons of Thunder."

As the Sons of Thunder approached the Stone to touch it, a barricade of law officers stood arm to arm in riot gear, opposing the motorcyclists, assuming they were intent on defacing the Stone.

At that moment, I took the parchment in my hand and folded it like a paper airplane. I then placed the photographs inside it and tossed it. It sailed over the heads of the officers. I knew that if the pictures and the promise were to touch the Stone, then the power would be released upon the Sons of Thunder. When the paper was one foot away from the monument, just before actually touching the Stone, my dream ended.

I believe this portrays the role of intercessory prayer in helping the Church get past the barricades of legalism, and open the gifts of God for reaching the lost with the message of Christ. The Sons of Thunder, represented by motorcyclists on the service road, illustrate the servant-heart of ministry. They also show the agility and decisiveness necessary in reaching the lost. The fact that they were in single file shows, in my opinion, the unity we must maintain as Christians in order for our message about Christ to have credibility.

Now, I extend to you a prayer God will capture your heart and bring you into full devotion to Christ Jesus; that your passion for music will be equalled by your love for the lost. I pray that you will receive an anointing from God to minister with artistic creativity that is so compelling in its quality, and in its message thousands of unbelievers who are lost in darkness will see the light and turn to Jesus to be cleansed and born again!